Fundamentals of the Structure and History of Russian

A Usage-Based Approach

FUNDAMENTALS OF THE STRUCTURE AND HISTORY OF RUSSIAN

A USAGE-BASED APPROACH

BY

DAVID K. HART AND
GRANT H. LUNDBERG

Bloomington, Indiana, 2013

SLAVICA

10073649327

ISBN 978-0-89357-396-6

Library of Congress Cataloging-in-Publication Data

Hart, David K., author.
  Fundamentals of the structure and history of Russian : a usage-based
approach / by David K. Hart and Grant H. Lundberg.
      pages ; cm
  Includes bibliographical references and index.
  ISBN 978-0-89357-396-6
  1. Russian language--Phonology. 2. Russian language--Morphology. 3.
  Russian language--Morphophonemics. I. Lundberg, Grant H., 1968- author.
  II. Title.
  PG2131.H37 2013
  491.75--dc23
                            2013035625

Slavica Publishers
Indiana University
1430 N. Willis Dr.
Bloomington, IN 47404-2146
USA

[Tel.] 1-812-856-4186
[Toll-free] 1-877-SLAVICA
[Fax] 1-812-856-4187
[Email] slavica@indiana.edu
[www] http://www.slavica.com/

Table of Contents

INTRODUCTION

> *Natural languages are fantastically vast, complex and mysterious systems whose principles have so far largely eluded specification.*
>
> — Paul Postal, "The Best Theory" (1972)

How do human languages work? How is it possible for anyone, let alone a two-year old child, to learn and ultimately master the virtually limitless intricacies of a language? Beyond vocabulary and grammar rules, what is it specifically that native speakers know that allows them to speak so fluently and effortlessly? No one ultimately knows the answers to these and similar language questions. Over the past several hundred years languages have been carefully dissected and theories about their composition have been worked out, each theory building on the "ruins" of a previous theory. Though progress has been made, Paul Postal's statement about the mysterious complexity and elusiveness of language continues to be true.

This text aims to assist the Russian learner understand the patterns and alternations in the sounds and structures of Russian, a language replete with complex alternations. For its framework, we use a type of linguistic analysis called "cognitive" or "usage-based" linguistics as found in the theoretical work of Langacker, Bybee, and others. This approach avoids traditional abstract underlying forms and ordered rules in favor of describing the language using only information available to native speakers. Words or variations of words are categorized and related by rule, but these are rules which emerge based on the patterns found in actually spoken words. Given the pervasiveness of writing today, we also consider how speech is represented graphically. Through this approach Russian sounds can be shown to behave in a very systematic way. Russian noun and adjective declension, while appearing chaotic, is actually quite orderly when seen in the light of a usage-based analysis. The same can be said for verbal inflection and even derivational morphology.

   This book is divided into three parts. Part I covers the fundamentals of Russian phonetics and phonology, and introduces the reader to how usage-based processes account for sound alternations. In Part II we discuss inflectional and derivational morphology and bring to bear questions whose answers up until now have eluded elegant explanation. Parts I and II (composed of chapters 1–6) make up the majority of the book. Taken together, they represent a coherent description of the interaction of sound and meaning in Russian. In Part III, we review the main historical developments that have produced the system described in Parts I and II. While it is useful to look at the history of a language in order to understand *why* the system operates as it does today, we are careful to distinguish historical language information (what may have been available to speakers at an earlier time) from information that is available to today's Russian speakers.

Part I

Russian Sounds

Why do foreigners have accents? For example, why do Russians learning English often mix up *w* and *v* when they speak English, or why do Japanese speakers sometimes have a hard time with the English letters *r* and *l*? English-speaking learners of Russian also usually speak Russian with an accent. Accents arise because each language has its own sound system. Each language has a set of sounds which may or may not overlap with those of other languages. Russian м, for example, is very similar to English *m*, but Russian has other sounds (i.e., ы) not found in English. English differentiates between *w* and *v*, while in the Russian alphabet there is no special letter for *w*, so Russians learning English sometimes pronounce both sounds as *v*, making *wail* sound more like *veil*. Similar problems plague English speakers learning Russian. For example, in Russian most consonants can be either "hard" or "soft." This distinction is difficult for English speakers to perceive and produce because "hard" and "soft" is not an important characteristic of English. Furthermore, accents may be "strong," or "hardly noticeable at all," or somewhere in between. Foreigners have accents because they are used to pronouncing sounds according to the system of their native language and import these pronunciation habits into their second language. Other reasons have to do with intonation, or the musical pitch, of words and sentences and the placement of stress.

The focus of Part I is on the Russian sound system. We will discuss how Russians produce speech sounds, how these sounds differ from similar sounds in English, and how they function as a system. While it is unlikely that readers will lose their foreign accent simply by working through these chapters, it is hoped that the principles set forth here will provide a foundation for practicing spoken Russian in a way which, in time, will aid the learner to have more native-like pronunciation.

Each chapter is composed of several sections which introduce topics dealing with pronunciation and which build on preceding sections.

We have found it very useful to use the text in conjunction with one-on-one practice with a native speaker. But even without a native speaker, the topics covered should provide any serious student of Russian with a basis for understanding how the Russian system of sounds works and how it differs from that of English.

CHAPTER 1

1.1. Letters and Sounds

Oddly enough, we begin our discussion of the sounds of Russian by examining some of the sounds of English and how they are represented in writing. English is famous—or infamous—for the inconsistencies of its spelling of words. For example, *live* (the verb) and *live* (the adjective, as in "Live from New York!") are pronounced differently. In these words the same letter -*i*- has two different pronunciations. In fact, English has 18 more sounds than it does letters. The letter *a* is another good example of a letter with multiple personalities. It represents the sound [a] as heard in *father*. But the letter *a* also represents other sounds, as in the first sound in the word *about*. This very short sound is called a schwa and it is symbolized by what looks like an upside down *e*: [ə]. Note that this sound does not equate to the *a* as it is pronounced in *father*. This is another example of how one letter can represent more than one sound. We can illustrate this situation using a chart or a schema, where the upper level represents a category and the lower level represents examples or members of that category:

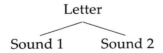

For example, the letter *a* represents pronunciations:

        [ə] (as in *about*)   [a] (as in *father*)

The English letter *a* has other pronunciations, too. Consider the pronunciation of *a* in the following words:

       cat   *ate*   *carriage*   *lawyer*

Most American speakers pronounce the *a* in each of these words differently, including the second *a* in *carriage* which is barely pronounced, if at all.

The inconsistencies of spelling and the multiplicity of sounds represented by a single letter present a problem for people learning to speak English. The opposite situation also occurs: a single sound can be represented by different letters. Consider, for example the first **sound** in the word *shall*. It is the *sh* sound. Note that English writing represents this sound in other ways, too:

submission   *machine*   *special*   *actually*

Thus, in English the sound *sh* is represented by letters

sh   *si*   *ch*   *ci*   *tu*

This characteristic of English accounts for the widespread existence of spelling bees in schools and spell checkers for computers.

We have seen two types of problems with the English alphabet. In the first, one letter represents multiple sounds. In the second, a single sound is represented by multiple letters. Both of these situations also occur in Russian, though not to the same degree as in English. To study pronunciation in a precise way, we need a system of writing where every letter corresponds to one sound only and vice versa:

Letter A   Sound 1
   | |
Sound 1   Letter A

The International Phonetic Alphabet (IPA) is just such a system and the sounds of many languages, including Russian, have been and are described using this system of mainly latin characters. However, most Russian linguists use a version of the Cyrillic alphabet to specify exactly how Russian words are pronounced. This is the system that we will use in this text and that we will introduce in the next section. All phonetic descriptions, however, have in common two things: (i) they all have a one-to-one correspondence of letter to sound and (ii) they all use square brackets to indicate that a phonetic system is being used, not just regular orthography, i.e., regular spelling. For example, the sound *sh* is rendered [š] in IPA, and as [ш] in the Russian phonetic alphabet. As we will see later, each symbol is exactly defined, so there can be no doubt as to what sound the symbol represents.

1.1.1. Phonetic Transcription (Фонети́ческая транскри́пция)

Consider the following explanation of writing Russian sounds phonetically:

> Для того, чтобы как можно точнее записать звучащую речь используют фонетическую транскрипцию. В фонетической транскрипции используют буквы традиционного алфавита, при этом запись ведётся по особым неорфографическим законам. Некоторые буквы не употребляют (*я, ё, е, ю*). Основной принцип фонетической транскрипции—строгое и однозначное соответствие буквами и звуками. Один знак и одна буква всегда обозначают один и тот же звук. Орфографическое письмо не всегда соответствует фонетическому.
>
> Основной принцип русской транскрипции реализуется в правилах:
>
> 1. употребление букв алфавита, используемых в транскрипции, только в соответствии со звучанием, а не по правилам орфографии;
> 2. мягкие согласные обозначаются теми же буквами, но с диакритическим знаком [’];
> 3. для обозначения йода используют [й];
> 4. буквы *я, ё, е, ю* не используются;
> 5. ъ и ь используются для обозначения редуцированных гласных (schwa);
> 6. обязательно обозначение ударения.
>
> [adapted from gumfak.ru]

The diacritic mark (*диакрити́ческий знак*) mentioned in number 2 to show soft consonants refers to a mark written above a given letter. In Russian phonetic transcription this is an apostrophe [’] for soft consonants. For example, Russian *иска́ть* is transcribed as [иска́т’], where the apostrophe indicates the *m* is soft. Why not just use a soft sign? Two reasons. First, as indicated in number 5 above, the hard sign and soft sign are recruited in Russian phonetic transcription to represent actual sounds in Russian for which there are no special letters. (We'll get to these sounds later.) Second, we want to have just one symbol to represent softness in consonants. Russian indicates softness in **writing** with letters other than the soft sign. Recall that Russian has ten vowel letters, but that these letters represent just six sounds:

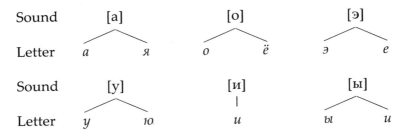

As indicated above, Russian has two **written letters** for each vowel sound (except [и], which we will discuss below). Why? One of the most important characteristics of Russian speech is the difference between hard and soft consonants. This difference is critical to normal Russian pronunciation and the improper control of hard and soft consonants immediately marks a foreign accent. This differentiation is so important that it is expressed in writing: a consonant is shown to be soft when followed by a soft sign or one of the letters *я, ё, е, ю, и*. This can be seen in the following transcriptions:

Written	represents	Spoken
иска́ть		[иска́т']
тю́бик		[т'у́б'ик]
мать		[мат']
твёрдый		[тв'о́рдый]
име́л		[им'э́л]
сел		[с'эл]
но́ги		[но́г'и]
пи́шут		[п'и́шут]
пять		[п'ат']

Note that softness is expressed only one way in phonetic transcription: by ['] following a consonant. Since softness is a feature of consonants only, the symbol ['] never follows a vowel and never occurs at the beginning of a word. Russian has three sounds that are **always soft**: ч, щ, й. Since these sounds are always soft, strange as it may seem, Russian linguists usually do not mark them with an apostrophe in phonetic transcription: [ч] [щ] [й]. This actually makes sense if we think of ['] being used only for consonants that can be either hard or soft. In this book we will follow the Russian way and not put an apostrophe after [ч], [щ], or [й].

Practice

A. What Russian words do the following phonetic transcriptions represent? Write out the words in normal orthography.

1. [с'áду]
2. [ступл'ý]
3. [стýп'ит]
4. [л'эт]
5. [з'имá]

6. [из'ýм]
7. [с'эл]
8. [йáрус]
9. [св'эт]
10. [йýный]

B. Write the following in phonetic transcription.

1. блéдный
2. включáть
3. где
4. гря́зный
5. слéдующий

6. член
7. жýткий
8. извиня́юсь
9. клён
10. чудéсный

C. Be prepared to read the following tongue twisters and joke out loud. Note how your pronunciation of hard consonants differs (or does not differ!!) from soft consonants.

1. Бык бодáется с быкóм.
   Убегáют все кругóм.
   Береги́, бегýн, бокá
   От бодли́вого быкá.

2. Не жалéла мáма мы́ла.
    Мáма Мúлу мы́лом мы́ла.
    Мúла мы́ла не любúла,
    мы́ло Мúла уронúла.

3. Сын — Пáпа, ты и тепéрь растёшь?
    Отéц — Почемý, ты дýмаешь, что я растý?
    Сын — А потомý, что у тебя́ макýшка стáла высó-
    вываться из волóс.

1.1.2. [й]

Exactly how Russians pronounce soft consonants, as opposed to hard
variants, is the topic of section 2.1. Right now we want to be sure we
know how to represent soft consonants in phonetic transcription. We
learned in the preceding section that soft consonants, for example, *ть*
or *тя*, are represented in **phonetic transcription** by a consonant followed by an apostrophe, e.g. [т'], [т'а]. In writing, both the soft sign
and the vowels *я, ё, ю, е, и* indicate preceding consonants are soft. But
what if these vowel letters don't follow a consonant? What if, instead,
they are at the beginning of a word, as in *éсли*, or they follow another
vowel, as in *сиять*? What sound do these letters represent in those
contexts?

The letters *я, ё, ю, е* are versatile in that they can show softness of
preceding consonants, or if no consonant precedes, they show the
presence of an [й] in the word. So instead of writing *сийать*, Russians
use *я*: *сиять* 'to shine', although the first would work just as well as
the second. Similarly, at the beginning of a word these four vowel letters represent the presence of an [й]: *ёлки* [йóлк'и], *ясный* [йáсный]. If
any of these four vowel letters **or the letter** *и* occurs after a hard sign
or soft sign, then the magical [й] is again present: *съел* 'he ate' [сйэл],
питьё [п'ит'йó]. In summary:

[й] is pronounced when

		written	pronounced
1.	*я, ё, ю, е* is after a vowel	мóю 'I wash'	[мóйу]
2.	*я, ё, ю, е* is at the beginning of a word	я́щик 'box'	[йáщик]

3.	*я, ё, ю, е,* or *и* is after a hard or soft sign	питьё 'drink'	[п'ит'йо́]
		съел 'he ate'	[сйэл]
		чьи 'whose'	[чйи]

Practice

A. Write out the following words in phonetic transcription:

1. лёг	6. тем	11. слюня́вый	16. лицо́
2. ля́гу	7. клюю́	12. судьба́	17. изба́
3. вёл	8. сто́ит	13. письмо́	18. свинья́
4. тётю	9. ю́жный	14. люблю́	19. грубия́н
5. мыть	10. нытьё	15. мёртвый	20. кро́ю

B. Write the following in normal orthography.

1. [взаи́мный]	6. [сыр'йо́]
2. [вызыва́йущий]	7. [чо́рный]
3. [в'йу́г'и]	8. [чуд'э́сный]
4. [вычисл'а́т']	9. [йа́щик'и]
5. [вручну́йу]	10. [гн'ил'йо́]

C. Be prepared to read the following out loud. Pay attention to the pronunciation of words with a hard or soft sign.

1. Се́ла мы́шка в уголо́к,
Съе́ла бу́блика кусо́к.

2. Зада́ли в шко́ле де́тям уро́к:
Пры́гают в по́ле со́рок соро́к.
Де́сять взлете́ли, се́ли не е́ли.
Ско́лько оста́лось в по́ле соро́к?

3. Объявле́ние на столбе́: «Экстрасе́нс. Лечу́ от всех боле́зней.» Ми́мо прохо́дит мужи́к и говори́т себе́ под нос: «Лети́, лети́, от всех не улети́шь!»

1.2. The Articulation of Consonants

Speech sounds are produced by means of the speech apparatus. Speech begins in the lungs which, when contracted, send a rush of air toward the oral cavity. As shown in the illustration below, the oral cavity involves a number of sound-forming instruments: the tongue, lips, teeth, the alveolar ridge (the hard ridge right behind the upper teeth), the hard palate, the soft palate, the tip of the tongue, the body of the tongue, the back part of the tongue, and the voice box. In addition, sound waves can be blocked in the mouth but continue to travel through the nasal cavity producing sounds such as an [м] and [н].

1. язы́к
2. гу́бы
3. зу́бы
4. альвео́лы
5. твёрдое нёбо
6. мя́гкое нёбо
7. ко́нчик языка́
8. носова́я по́лость
9. голосовы́е свя́зки

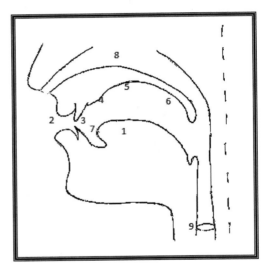

By creating different kinds of obstructions to the airflow coming from the lungs, speakers are able to create a variety of sounds. Obstruction to the airflow can be accomplished in various ways. For example, the airflow can be stopped completely by closing the lips briefly and then opening them again to produce a [п] sound. We characterize or "define" individual sounds simply by indicating where in the speech apparatus they are formed. The sound [п] is a "labial" (*губно́й*) sound, created by closing the lips. What other "labial" sounds are there in Russian? Try pronouncing the following consonants (*согла́сные*). Which ones represent labials (which sounds do you use your lips to make)?

т   к   г   в   м   с   р   н   п   ш   ф   б

There are actually only three letters above that represent true labials. Two others are labial-dentals (the upper teeth contact the lower lips), namely [в] and [ф]. But we will classify the labial-dentals also as labials:

labials: [м] [п] [б] [в] [ф]

Russian has other groupings of sounds based on **place of articulation** (*ме́сто артикуля́ции*), that is, where in the speech apparatus the sound is produced:

labial   pronounced LAY-bee-ul (see above)

dental   (*зубно́й*): the tip of the tongue touches or comes extremely close to the back of the teeth

palatal   (*нёбный*): the body of the tongue touches or comes very near to the roof of the mouth, the hard palate; includes [й] where the body of the tongue starts close to the roof of the mouth and is then slightly lowered

velar,   pronounced vEElur, (*задненёбный*): the back part of the tongue touches or comes extremely close to the soft palate

---

Practice

A. Define each group of sounds as to where they are produced in the speech apparatus.

    1. м   п   б   в   ф   *губны́е*

    2. к   г   х   _____

    3. й   _____

    4. т   д   с   з   л   н   ц   _____

    5. ч   ш   ж   _____

B. Read the following out loud.

> Говори́т попуга́й попуга́ю:
> "Я тебя́, попуга́й, попуга́ю".
> Отвеча́ет ему́ попуга́й:
> "Попуга́й меня́, попуга́й!"

> Бе́лый снег. Бе́лый мел.
> Бе́лый са́хар то́же бел.
> А вот бе́лка не бела́.
> Бе́лой да́же не была́.

1.2.1. Voice

We saw earlier that the difference between hard and soft consonants is critical in speech. The difference between voiced and voiceless conso-nants is just as important. Consider, for example, the sounds [c] and [з]. Both are dentals, but obviously they differ in an important way because words such as *сон* 'sleep, dream' and *зон* 'zones (gen pl)' clearly sound differently. The difference between them is that [c] is voiceless and [з] is voiced. To create a voiced (*зво́нкий*) consonant, speakers produce the consonant and at the same time cause the vocal chords to vibrate. The sound [c] is voiceless (*глухо́й*) because the vocal chords are not vibrating when it is produced. The sounds [н], [м], [л], [р], and [й] form a subset of voiced consonants: the sonorants. As shown below, they do not have voiceless counterparts:

VOICED

[б] [в] [з] [д] [ж] [г] [м] [н] [р] [л] [й]
.... (sonorants)

VOICELESS

[п] [ф] [с] [т] [ш] [к] [х] [ц] [ч] [щ]
.... (*)

The first six sounds in each list are paired consonants—they come in voiced/voiceless pairs. Read each pair out loud. The sonorants (*соно́рные*) are special in that they do not have voiceless counterparts.

The final four voiceless sounds listed above (marked *) are special in that, though they have voiced counterparts, the Russian alphabet has no letter for them. More on this later.

1.2.2. Manner of Articulation

If [c] and [т] are both voiceless dentals, how can we differentiate between them? Consider the following description by one of Russia's leading phoneticians:

> Различия между согласными зависят не только от наличия или отсутствия голоса или места образования, но также и от **способа** образования преграды. Согласные по способу образования делятся на **смычные, аффрикаты, и щелевые**. При образовнии смычных согласных образуется полное смыкание (затвор). При образовании щелевых согласных образуется узкая щель, шум образуется в результате трения выдыхаемого воздуха о стенки щели. Такие звуки называются также фрикативными. При образовании аффрикат образуется полное смыкание, но размыкание происходит не мгновенно, а путем перехода смыкания в щель. Сонорные по способу образования могут быть щелевыми ([й]), проходными ([м], [н], [л]), и дрожащим ([р]).
>
> (Р. И. Аванесов)

Two important characteristics of consonants have to do with voice (voiced, voiceless) and with place of articulation (labial, dental, etc.). Here Avanesov speaks of a third critical way of distinguishing consonants: their means (*способ*) of articulation. He speaks of four:

stop (*смы́чный*)	п	б	т	д	к	г
fricative (*щелево́й*)	ф	в	с	з	х	ш ж
affricate (*аффрика́та*)	ц	ч	(щ)			
sonorant (*соно́рный*)	м	н	л	р	й	

With **stops** the airflow is stopped completely but momentarily, such as with the sounds [т] and [д]. With **fricatives** the airflow is restricted so a hushing sound occurs, as in the sounds [ш] and [ж]. The **affricates** are a combination of stop+fricative, as in [ц] and [ч], essentially these sounds are [тс] and [т′ш′]. In standard Moscow pronunciation щ is a soft fricative [ш′], in St. Petersburg, it ends in a slight affricate [ч] sound. Avanesov points out that sonorants can be fricative ([й]), continuous ([м], [н], [л]), or trilled ([р]). We differentiate the continuous sonorants by noting that [м] is a labial nasal sonorant, [н] is a dental nasal sonorant, and [л] is a dental oral sonorant.

Consonants can be characterized uniquely by reference to place and manner of articulation and voicing quality. For example,

[т] can be "defined" as a **voiceless, dental stop**

No other sound has this definition. Similarly we recognize [д] as a **voiced, dental stop.** The only difference between [д] and [т], theoretically, is that one is voiced the other voiceless. These two sounds are otherwise identical as to place and manner of articulation. Note that in English at the beginning of words voiceless stops are accompanied with a tiny puff of air (aspiration): tack [tʰæk], peel [pʰīl] as opposed to Russian which does not have aspiration: *так, пил* [так], [п′ил].

Practice

A. Which sounds are described? Write down the corresponding Russian letter, and then, using the chart below, translate the definition into Russian.

1.	voiceless	dental	stop
2.	voiced	labial	stop
3.	voiceless	velar	stop
4.	voiceless	labial	fricative
5.	voiceless	palatal	fricative
6.	voiced	palatal	fricative
7.	voiced	labial	sonorant
8.	voiced	dental	trill
9.	voiced	dental	oral sonorant
10.	voiced	dental	nasal sonorant

B. Write the voice, place, and manner of articulation of the following:

1. [б]   6. [г]
2. [п]   7. [х]
3. [т]   8. [к]
4. [с]   9. [д]
5. [ж]   10. [в]

C. Pronounce the following Russian-English word pairs. What differences do you notice in the place and manner of articulation of the initial consonant?

1. пять – pat   3. тот – tote
2. кит – kit   4. дом – dome

The following charts out the relationships between consonant sounds for which Russian has letters.

МЕСТО И СПОСОБ АРТИКУЛЯЦИИ

препятствующие	губной	зубной	небный	задненебный
глухой смычный	п-п′	т-т′		к
звонкий смычный	б-б′	д-д′		г
глухой щелевой	ф-ф′	с-с′	ш	х
звонкий щелевой	в-в′	з-з′	ж	
глухая аффриката		ц	ч	
сонорные				
носовой	м-м′	н-н′		
боковой		л-л′		
дрожащий		р-р′		
глайд			й	

We can see that the relationship between, say, [п] and [б] is one of voice. But that is the limit of their relationship. One is not a variant of another. The two sounds exist independently of each other. They are both labials, one voiced, one voiceless:

[LABIAL STOP]
/   \
[п]   [б]
voiceless   voiced

This is an important concept because we want to consider word pairs such as *пал* 'he fell' and *бал* 'ball' as words completely independent of each other. They are **unrelated** to each other in every way except that they happen to rhyme. In other words, the [п] in *пал* does not come from the [б] in *бал*, and vice versa. We term *пал-бал* "minimal pairs" in that they differ phonetically very slightly, only by the feature of voice, but this is enough to trigger a differentiation of meaning in these words!

1.3. Articulation of Vowels

The oral cavity can be considered as a more or less oval (on its side) resonating chamber. By moving the tongue around in this chamber a variety of timbres (vowels) can be produced. By dividing the mouth up into five areas, we can characterize each vowel as to which area, more or less, it is produced in. Each area contains several vowels, and each vowel is represented by two areas:

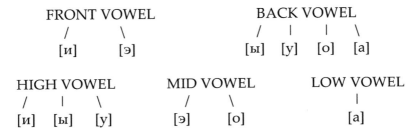

In addition to being produced in the front of the mouth or the back of the mouth, vowels can also be characterized as being produced high in the mouth, low in the mouth, or in the middle range. Reference to high, mid, low, front, and back is to the relative location of the tongue when producing these vowels.

By referring to these five areas of the oral cavity we can uniquely characterize each vowel:

и	high	front	vowel
э	mid	front	vowel
ы	high	back	vowel
у	high	back	vowel (rounded)
о	mid	back	vowel
а	low	back	vowel

Note that we must add the feature "rounded" (*кру́глый*) to differentiate between the two high back vowels [у] and [ы]. The reference is to the rounded lips that accompany the production of [у].

Practice

A. Characterize each of the vowels above in Russian.

B. What is the main difference between the following pairs of vowels?

и	э
и	ы
э	о
у	о
и	а

C. Name the vowel that is

1. сре́дний за́дний гла́сный   [   ]
2. высо́кий пере́дний гла́сный   [   ]
3. сре́дний пере́дний гла́сный   [   ]
4. ни́зкий за́дний гла́сный   [   ]

D. What pronunciation feature(s) do the following sound pairs have in common (answer in Russian):

1. [о] [э]
2. [и] [э]
3. [о] [а]
4. [и] [у]
5. [а] [ы]
6. [м] [н]
7. [т] [к]
8. [с] [ж]
9. [л] [д]
10. [а] [б]

E. Read the following out loud.

—Что ты натвори́л! Ты же заби́л мяч в свои́ воро́та!
—Не удержа́лся, така́я удо́бная пози́ция была́.

2.1. Introduction

Earlier we discussed a way to represent sounds by written symbols using phonetic transcription: one sound—one symbol. We also defined the sounds of Russian using articulatory features. Anyone who has studied Russian knows that one of its fundamental characteristics is that the pronunciation of words may differ when conjugated or declined in the various cases. For example, in *волна́* 'wave' the first vowel, though it is written as an *o*, is pronounced something more like an *a*. But in the nom pl an [o] sound is pronounced *во́лны* [во́лны] 'waves'. The two pronunciations of written *o* in these words represent two parts of an alternation (*чередова́ние*). Much of the rest of this book is concerned with describing the relationship between different kinds of alternations. In this chapter, we will deal with phonetic alternations, that is alternations in sounds alone. We will be particularly interested in knowing what RULES of pronunciation there are, so that we can tune our own speaking to these rules.

2.2. What is a Hard Consonant and a Soft Consonant?

Russian makes a critical distinction between "hard" and "soft" consonants. The terms "hard" and "soft" are not based in articulation, but more in how these consonants sound when they are pronounced. Here is what Avanesov has to say about the difference in pronunciation of consonants that are paired for hardness and softness.

Твердые и мягкие согласные

Одной из самых характерных особенностей звуковой системы русского языка является различение твердых и мягких согласных. Большая часть согласных употребляется в русском языке как в твердом, так и в мягком виде. В речи русских эта норма редко нарушается. Однако она нередко с трудом дается нерусским—представителям как народов [бывшего] Советского Союза, так и зарубежных. Поэтому при изучении русского языка нерусским особенно серьезное внимание уделить произношению мякгих согласных в противоположность твердым.

Чтобы правильно произносить мягкие согласные русского языка, надо знать, как они образуются в отличие от твердых согласных. При образовании мягкгого согласного язык занимает положение, близкое к тому, в котором он бывает при произношении [и] или [й], т. е. средняя часть спинки языка высоко поднимается к соответствующей части нёба. Твердые согласные образуются без этой дополнительной 'йотовой' артикуляции. Это можно легко заметить, произнося твердые и мягкие пары согласных [т] и [т'], [с] и [с'], [л] и [л'].   (Аванесов 100–01)

Practice

A. Given the definition of hard/soft consonants above, determine which line in each of the following represents a hard or soft consonant. Pronounce each of the sounds several times as you do this exercise, and take note of the location of your tongue. (Drawings are from the 1980 Russian Academy Grammar.)

Which line represents [к] as in *кот* and which represents [к'] as in *кит*?

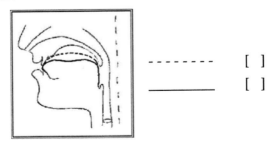

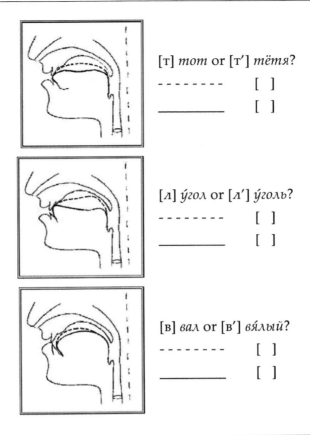

[т] *тот* or [т'] *тётя?*

- - - - - - - -   [ ]

_____   [ ]

[л] *ýгол* or [л'] *ýголь?*

- - - - - - - -   [ ]

_____   [ ]

[в] *вал* or [в'] *вя́лый?*

- - - - - - - -   [ ]

_____   [ ]

2.2.1. Hard Consonant ~ Soft Consonant Alternation

The hard ~ soft distinction occurs only with consonants. Sometimes softness is called "palatalization" (*палатализа́ция*), because the tongue is raised toward the hard palate when pronouncing soft consonants. In a strictly linguistic sense, it is *incorrect* to speak of "hard" or "soft" vowels, since there are no hard or soft variants of vowels (see chapter one). The vowels that are pronounced with the tongue raised high and slightly pushed forward ([и] and [э]) are sometimes mistakenly called "soft" vowels. We refer to them simply as "front" vowels. Similarly we don't want to refer to vowel *letters* as soft or hard: *ю, е, ё, и, я* are not soft vowels or soft letters. They are simply letters that show that a preceding consonant is soft (*мять* [м'ат'] 'crumple') or that the preceding consonant is [й], as at the beginning of a word: *ест* [йэст] 'eats'.

Practice

A. Read the following out loud. Notice where the sound [й] appears. Notice the difference in your pronunciation between soft and hard consonants.

1. путь	6. я́сный	11. месть	16. мыл
2. тут	7. кол	12. ти́хий	17. ча́шки
3. брат	8. боль	13. тёти	18. ша́шки
4. брать	9. мост	14. тот	19. ёлки
5. ей	10. мест	15. мил	20. я́ркий

B. Write the words in A in phonetic transcription.

The distinction between hard and soft consonants is so important, that it is shown in the way words are spelled.

Мягкие и твердые согласные в русском языке различаются в следующих положениях:

1. На конце слова и перед некоторыми согласными. Мягкость обознается буквой *ь*: *печать, сталь, письмо, просьба*. Буква *ь* после шипящих (*ш, ж, ч, щ*) никакого указания на произношение не заключает, так как звуки [ш] и [ж] произносятся всегда твердо, а звуки [й], [ч], и [щ]—всегда мягко.

2. Перед гласными [а], [у], [о]. В этом положении мягкость обозначается буквами *я, ю, ё*: *мял, тянут, люди, нёс*. В русском языке все согласные (кроме *ж, ш, ц*) перед гласными на месте [и] или [э] произносятся мягко: *вилка, мил, дикий, руки, хитрый, тебе, руке, тесно, белый*. Однако заднеязычные ([к], [г], [х]) всегда произносятся твердо перед гласными на месте [а], [у], и [о].

3. Гласный [ы] в начале слова в русских словах не встречается: он употребляется в положении после твердого согласного: *опыт, бык, тыл, дым, мышь*. После твердых шипящих [ш] и [ж], а также

обычно после [ц] он обозначается буквой *и*: жир [жыр], шить [шыт'], цирк [цырк]. После твердых представок встречается *ы* [ы] на письме:

игра́ть ~ сыгра́ть   иду́щий ~ предыду́щий
иска́ть ~ взыска́ть   интере́сный ~ безынтере́сный

(Avanesov)

We have seen that most consonants in Russian come in pairs as to hardness and softness. In other words they can be either hard or soft. For example, the sound represented by the letter л can be hard or soft, as seen in the words у́гол 'corner' and у́голь 'coal'. Since л can be hard or soft, we say that it is a paired consonant (it comes in a pair: [л] and [л']). However, not all consonants are paired for hardness/softness. Some, as indicated by Avanesov in paragraph 1 above, are always soft, namely [й], [ч], and [щ]. Since these consonants are always soft Russian linguists normally do not mark them with an apostrophe, which is reserved for soft-paired consonants. Other consonants are always hard, namely [ж], [ш], and [ц]. No matter what letter might follow these in writing (including the soft sign!), they are always pronounced hard. So we say that these six consonants are unpaired, they do not come in pairs.

2.2.2. Writing, Pronunciation, and Rules

People can speak without knowing how to write, such as children who normally learn to speak long before they learn to read and write. However, writing, especially for nonnative students of Russian, is an indispensable tool in the learning process. In fact, we often encounter words for the first time in written form. So it can be helpful to develop pronunciation rules based on the written language. In other words, we want to be able to go from writing to phonetic transcription and back again.

While Russian writing represents pronunciation fairly well (much better than English writing represents English pronunciation), it still is not a completely accurate representation. For example, it does not always follow a one-to-one correspondence between letter and sound. However, when used together with pronunciation rules, it becomes an extremely accurate method of representing the pronunciation of Russian words.

Before we tackle pronunciation rules in Russian, it will be useful to look at how they are written. In this course, rules simply tell what is, what can be observed. Our rules do not suggest what sounds turn into what, or anything like that. We simply state what sounds go together, using the sequence YZ, where Y is one sound or a phonetic environment and Z is another sound. Sometimes we will use the sequence, X: YZ, where the italic X represents a written letter, Y is a sound or phonetic environment and Z is a sound.

For example, consider the pronunciation of stressed -e- before soft consonants. A very distinct sound alternation can be heard in the pronunciation of stressed [э] when it precedes a soft consonant. Avanesov states, "В положении перед мягким согласным гласный [э] звучит закрыто, узко." Avanesov describes this sound as "closed, narrow." We will adopt the traditional English terminology for this sound: "tense e." This is somewhat similar to the English sound -ay- in words like _ache_ and _ate,_ only shorter and with the mouth closed even more for the Russian sound. We will transcribe this sound as [ê]. Compare, for example, the pronunciation of -e- in the following pairs:

болéл [э]	болéли [ê]
дéло [э]	на сáмом дéле [ê]
свéт [э]	свéтит [ê]
сдéлал [э]	здесь [ê]

We describe this pronunciation phenomenon by means of a rule:

(1) Tense "e" rule $é : [ê]C'$ (where C' = soft consonant)

This rule states that stressed _e_, when followed by a soft consonant, is pronounced [ê].

Practice

A. Read the following words out loud. Use the 'Tense "e" rule' where appropriate.

1. век
2. билéт
3. билéте (prep sg)

4. газéта
5. газéте (prep sg)
6. музéй

7. вéчный   9. двéсти

8. две   10. вещь

B. Write the words in A in phonetic transcription.

2.2.3. The Yeri Rule

The letter *ы* is commonly called by its sound [ы]. In Avanesov's discussion of this sound (paragraph 3 of section 2.2.1), he states that it occurs only after hard consonants. We can restate this information using convenient symbols:

(2) C″[ы]   (C″ = hard consonant)

The rule in (2) states that the sound [ы] occurs after hard consonants.

The second part of paragraph 3 indicates that after the consonants [ш], [ж], and [ц]) the sound [ы] is expressed by the written letter *и*! We represent this as:

(3) *и*: ж, ш, ц [ы]

The rule in (3) states that written *и* is pronounced as [ы] after the letters indicated. While this may seem surprising, in fact it makes a lot of sense in terms of speech production, where, for the sake of simplicity, a sound takes on one or more characteristics of its neighbor. This process, known as assimilation, is discussed in more detail in section 2.4. Here the letter *и*, which normally represents the front vowel [и] instead represents the **back** vowel [ы] when it follows a hard, i.e., **back**, consonant: ж, ш, ц.

Now consider the final part of paragraph 3. It says that instead of *и*, we find written *ы* after "hard prefixes" (*твёрдые приставки*), as in *игрáть ~ сыгрáть*. By "hard prefixes" reference is to the final (hard) consonant of prefixes, such as in *с-, из-, раз-, от-*, etc. The alternation of *и* and *ы* after a hard prefix is similar to the process in (3), only in addition to being pronounced, *ы* is also written: *игрáть ~ сыгрáть*. This is really just another dimension of rule (2). This rule simply reminds us of why we see a shift in spelling in these circumstances. We combine the two rules (2) and (3) into one rule:

(4) Yeri rule: и: ж, ш, ц [ы]
                    C″[ы]   (where C″ is a hard consonant)

The rule in (4) states that written *и* is pronounced [ы] after hard consonants. Here is the "spelling" rule involving the spelling of *и* after hard prefixes:

(5)   *и*: C″[ы] (where C″ is the final consonant of a prefix)

Practice

A. Write the following in phonetic transcription. Include stress in multisyllabic words. Don't forget to apply the Yeri rule in your phonetic transcriptions. Read each word out loud.

1. чи́стый	6. сыгра́ть
2. глушь	7. мышь
3. живо́т	8. цикл
4. лю́льки	9. лы́жи
5. щи	10. де́ньги

B. Write the following in normal Russian orthography. Read each word out loud.

1. [к′ино́]	11. [кл′о́н]
2. [п′эч′]	12. [жыво́й]
3. [чи́щу]	13. [но́г′и]
4. [рук′и́]	14. [рук′э́]
5. [шол]	15. [цэн]
6. [чита́йут]	16. [п′ат′]
7. [жон]	17. [бо́л′шый]
8. [д′эт′и]	18. [н′икто́]
9. [тучо́к]	19. [йа́сный]
10. [ид′о́т]	20. [дружы́т′]

C. Read the following word pairs out loud. Pay attention to the pronunciation of hard and soft **consonants**. Can **you** hear a difference?

мил	грози́	сад
мыл	грозы́	деся́тый
пита́ть	мыл	стул
пыта́ть	мыль	утю́г
бить	шуми́т	нот
быть	мыт	гнёт
пуши́стый	ста́рший	у́жин
чи́стый	рабо́чий	грузи́н

2.2.4. The Soft Consonant Rule

Sooner or later most Russian learners notice that there are patterns in the Russian sound system. For example, as we saw above, the back vowel [ы] is always preceded by a hard consonant. This leads us to the next question—can we predict when the consonants will be hard or soft? The Soft Consonant rule answers this question: whenever a paired consonant occurs before a front vowel [э] (or its variant [э̂]) or [и], then it is soft. For example:

(6) де́ти   [д'э̂т'и]

In (6) the softness of the [д] and [т] can be predicted from the presence of [э̂] and [и]. At some level Russians know this phonetic reality; they know that paired consonants are always soft before the front vowels because they have seen, pronounced, and heard these combinations millions of times. In fact, it is a natural combination: soft consonants are fronted (see section 2.2.1) and so they naturally go along with front vowels. We express the Soft Consonant rule in the following way:

(7) Soft Consonant Rule: C′v̈   (where C = any paired consonant and v̈ = any front vowel)

According to the rule in (7) we can expect soft consonants to occur before front vowels. Note that the opposite is not true. We can't say that paired consonants are always hard before back vowels—there are a lot of words where a back vowel is preceded by a soft consonant, as in, for example, *Пётр* [п'отр]. We will learn why this is the case later; for now it's important to understand the relationship exhibited in (7). Paired consonants are always soft when they precede a front vowel, namely [э], [ə̂], and [и].

Note that the rule in (7) does not state that paired consonants switch from hard to soft. It just describes an observable feature of Russian pronunciation, not some process involving a change. So in *рукá*, the к is hard. In *рукé* the к is soft. Obviously the two words are related but one doesn't come from the other. We simply explain the [к] ~ [к'] relationship observed in these words by the rule in (2).

2.2.5. The Velars

Recall that paired consonants can be either hard or soft, while unpaired can be only hard or only soft. What about the velars, [к], [г], [х]? Consider the words below.

(8) кит   [к'ит]   конь   [кон']
     рукé   [рук'ə̂]   худóй   [худóй]
     гóрький   [гóр'к'ий]   гáснуть   [гáснут']
     хи́трый   [х'и́трый]   хор   [хор]

In this section we want to ask if there is a rule that expresses a relationship between hard and soft velars and the vowels they occur with. Velars are paired consonants, so we would expect the Soft Consonant rule to describe the situation with velars in the first column. Velars, however, are a little different. Recall that regular paired consonants are soft before front vowels, but can also be soft before back vowels (*Пётр*). In a sense, velars are purists. Soft velars only ever occur before front vowels, almost never (there is one exception) before back vowels. This is born out by the data in (8). Thus:

The sequence **hard velar + vowel** implies the vowel will always be [a], [y], or [o].

The sequence **soft velar + vowel** implies the vowel will always be [и], [э], or [ə̂].

In other words, the velars are like the paired consonants in that they are always soft before front vowels, but unlike paired consonants, they are always **hard** before back vowels. In linguistic terms, we can say that the velars are in *complementary distribution*, which simply means that one sound occurs in circumstance A, but never occurs in circumstance B, whereas another related sound always occurs in circumstance B, but never in A. The hard velars always occur before back vowels, and never before front vowels. The soft velars always occur before front vowels, and never before back vowels. Hard and soft velars are in complementary distribution. Since the orthography accurately represents this state of affairs, we do not need a pronunciation rule to express it. However, it is important for us to be aware of this relationship:

(9) Velars: K'v̆ (where K=any velar and v̆=front vowel)

  K"v̆ (where K"=any velar and v̆=back vowel)

The formulation in (9) represents the complementary distribution of hard/soft velars.

We see that the velars come in two variants each, hard and soft. However, these variants don't just occur without rhyme or reason, i.e., there is a real phonetic relationship between them. What does this mean in practice? When learners of Russian speak Russian but do not incorporate this relationship into their speech, they will be speaking with an accent. The more completely we are able to incorporate the relationships and patterns of the Russian sound system into our speech, the closer we will be to speaking as natives speak.

Practice

A. Pronounce the following Russian and English words. Be sure to keep in mind the complementary distribution between hard/soft velars. As you pronounce these words, you should be able to notice a different position of the tongue in Russian as opposed to English for the initial consonant in each word.

тел	tell	лист	list
мил	meal	крест	crest

тем	ten	дел	dell
нет	net	кем	chem
кий	key	гирь	gear

Another way to express the information discussed in this section is in a matrix.

(10)	before [a], [o], [y]	before [и], [э]	written
	[к]	[к′]	к
/VELARS/	[г]	[г′]	г
	[x]	[x′]	x

This matrix represents information known by native speakers of Russian. They have intuited this information by hearing and speaking thousands of combinations of sounds. When a sequence of sounds involving velars is presented to a native speaker and the sequence is not authorized by this network, then it is deemed to be incorrect in some way. For example, the sequence [x′и] and [к′э] are authorized, while the sequence [x′o] is not. Similarly, given the relations expressed above, we would never expect a written к to represent the sound [т]. The matrix does not authorize that relationship.

The Tense "e" rule, the Yeri rule, the Soft Consonant rule, and the information about velars represent observable language phenomena. Russians know this information. They use it every time they speak or listen. The matrix outlines accepted pronunciation norms for contemporary standard Russian. For example, upon hearing the sequence [ки], Russians know that they are dealing with a foreigner or someone who has trouble speaking normal Russian. That sequence never occurs in the standard language.

Practice

B. Tell whether or not the following phonetic sequences are found in Russian.

1. [к'и]   6. [м'о]
2. [кы]   7. [жы]
3. [дэ]   8. [то]
4. [м'ы]   9. [су]
5. [ши]   10. [чу]

C. Read the following out loud.

Встре́титься Змей и Змея́ захоте́ли.
Встре́титься Змей и Змея́ не суме́ли.
Змей в облака́х, а Змея́ на земле́.
На́до бы Зме́ю спусти́ться к Зме́е.

(М.Б. Успенский)

На́ша река́ широка́, как Ока́.
Как Ока́, широка́ на́ша река́.
Так, как Ока́, широка́ на́ша река́.

Ма́ленький Во́вочка не хо́чет спать. Оте́ц сади́тся у его́ крова́тки и начина́ет расска́зывать ему́ ска́зки. Расска́зывает час, друго́й. Наконе́ц в ко́мнате воцаря́ется тишина́. Мать ти́хо приоткрыва́ет дверь и спра́шивает:

—Он усну́л?

—Да, ма́ма, — шёпотом отвеча́ет сын.

2.3. Unstressed Vowels

Proper reduction of unstressed vowels is critical to sounding Russian-like. The vowels [и, у, ы] when unstressed are pronounced much like their stressed counterparts, only somewhat shorter. In phonetic transcription they are simply written without the stress mark, e.g., лю́ди [л'у́д'и]. The vowels [о, а, э] when unstressed, however, are pronounced differently from their stressed counterparts. In this section, we will concentrate on these.

2.3.1. Unstressed [a] and [o]

In the following quote the Russian phonetician, Julija Lebedeva, explains how *a* and *o* are pronounced depending on their position relative to the beginning of the word or to the stressed syllable:

> В начале слова и в первом предударном слоге после твердых согласных *о* и *а* звучат одинаково, как [ʌ]—это краткий, слабый [a]. В остальных безударных слогах *о, а* произносятся как [ъ], это более краткий и слабый [a].

The sound [ʌ] is similar to [a] but is somewhat laxer, shorter, and the tongue is not as low. Read the following words out loud and compare the pronunciation of the unstressed *o* and *a* with the stressed vowel next to it.

(11) гроза́   [грʌза́]   борьба́   [бʌр'ба́]

      мольба́   [мʌл'ба́]   поля́   [пʌл'а́]

      сосна́   [сʌсна́]   сова́   [сʌва́]

As explained above, *o* and *a* can be pronounced in an extremely reduced way, to where the vowel sound almost disappears. This happens when the vowel *o* or *a* is located after the stress or two or more syllables before the stress (but not in word initial position). We transcribe this very reduced sound as [ъ] (schwa). In (12) the reduction of [o] and [a] occurs based on the following distributions:

(i)	under stress	[o] [a]
(ii)	word initial	[ʌ]
(iii)	immediately before the stress	[ʌ]
(iv)	elsewhere	[ъ]

(12)

молоко́	[мълла́кó]	го́лову	[гóлъву]
вагóн	[вагóн]	обжóра	[лбжóръ]
молокосóс	[мълъклсóс]	сковорóды	[сковвъръды]
сковорода́	[скъвърлда́]	гóродом	[гóръдъм]
рабóта	[рлбóтъ]	за́пах	[за́пъх]
головá	[гълла́ва]	я́блоко	[йа́блъкъ]
одногó	[лдна́вó]	ти́хо	[т'и́хъ]
островá	[лстрла́ва́]	нóвой	[нóвъй]
магази́н	[мъглз'и́н]	хожу́	[хлжу́]

The pronunciation of these words is representative of akanje (а́канье). Notice that in each instance the sounds [л] and [ъ] follow a hard consonant. Reduction also takes place after soft consonants. This is known as ikanje (и́канье) and is discussed in 2.4.

2.3.2. Written Forms

If [л] and [ъ] stand for unstressed *o* **and** unstressed *a*, how can you tell which one, *o* or *a*, the reduced sound represents? Given an unfamiliar word, perhaps such as [клъдлвóй], how can we tell which vowel sound the [ъ] represents in writing, *клодовóй* or *кладовóй*? Technically there is no way to tell; either one is possible. Russian speakers do have a sense, however, of what vowel the reduced variant is likely to be related to. For example, in [клъдлвóй], native speakers know that the sequence [кл...д] probably represents the root -*клад*- as in *клад, склад, доклад* (all with a stressed -*a*-). The fact that Russian lacks the root *-клод*- supports this deduction. Literate native speakers also know that the adjective suffix and ending -*вóй* is normally preceded by the letter o or e, making the suffix either -*ов*- or -*ев*-. But for some unfamiliar words even native speakers may have trouble spelling the word correctly: [пърлшкóвый] → *порошкóвый* 'powdery'. A rhyme for Russian children learning to spell goes:

> Безуда́рный гла́сный звук,
> разберёшься с ним не вдруг:
> горá, моря́, травá, делá—
> как пра́вильно писа́ть словá?
> Чтóбы не бы́ло сомне́ния,

ста́вьте звук под ударе́ние:
го́ры, мо́ре, тра́вы, де́ло,
а тепе́рь пиши́те сме́ло!

(Бетенькова, 44)

This rhyme teaches that if you are not sure about the spelling, find a related form of the word where the questionable vowel is stressed. Then you can spell the word correctly.

2.3.3. Akanje

Some foreign speakers of Russian are content to pronounce unstressed [o] as [a] and unstressed [a] as [a], paying no attention to the further degrees of reduction discussed above, pronouncing, for example, молоко́ as *[малако́] or *[млλко́]. It is critical for proper standard Russian speech to pay attention to all three levels of pronunciation:

[o] [a]	full vowel	occurs under stress
[ʌ]	weaker	word initial or right before stress
[ъ]	very weak	unstressed positions

This is important in listening as well. The vowel [ъ] is sometimes so weak as to almost disappear from rapid speech: [млʌко́]. These articulatory relationships can be stated as a pronunciation rule based on the written language and on stress.

(13)   The Akanje Rule

unstressed *a, o*: #[ʌ], C″[ʌ]v́
              C″[ъ] elsewhere   (where C″=hard consonant
                                    and #=word boundary)

The rule in (13) states that unstressed *a* and *o* represent the sound [ʌ] when they occur at word initial position and when they occur right before the stress. Everywhere else these letters represent schwa [ъ].

Practice

A. Write the following in phonetic transcription:

1. коро́ва
2. ча́сто
3. друго́го
4. городо́к
5. вы́работать

6. старика́
7. голова́
8. сковорода́
9. сто́рону
10. огурцы́

B. Write the following in normal orthography. If you are not sure if the reduced vowel represents a written *o* or *a*, try to find a form of the word where stress falls on that vowel, or ask what the root, prefix or suffix might be.

1. [късмлл'о́т]
2. [бллту́н]
3. [зълътлцв'э́т]
4. [к'инъпънлра́мъ]
5. [грлма́днъст']

6. [то́пл'ивъ]
7. [нлга́]
8. [слсна́]
9. [лснлва́т']
10. [върлва́т']

C. Read the following out loud.

Звоно́к по телефо́ну: «Алло́! Я ваш сосе́д све́рху. Ско́лько мо́жно! Неме́дленно прекрати́те ва́ше пили́канье. Е́сли э́то пили́канье и да́льше бу́дет продолжа́ться, у меня́ кры́ша съе́дет!» — «Уже́ съе́хала. Скри́пку прода́ли неде́лю наза́д.»

2.3.4. Vowel Alternations

Consider the pairs:

(14) пал – бал   where [п] and [б] are similar: both are labial stops

(15) де́ло – те́ло   where [д] and [т] are similar: both are dental stops

(16) том – там   where [о] and [а] are similar: both are back vowels

The pairs of similar sounds in (14–16) stand out in that they are capable of changing the meaning of a word. Use [п] with the sequence [ал] and we have one word; use [б] with the same sequence and we have another word! **A sound that can change the meaning of a word in this way is called a phoneme (*фонéма*).** We will have more to say about phonemes later.

What about the pair of similar sounds in the following words:

(17) волнá – вóлны   where [ʌ] and [o] are similar: both are back vowels

(18) главá – глáвы   where [ʌ] and [a] are similar: both are back vowels

Sounds that alternate in predictable environments in one word but do not independently change the meaning of the word are called **allophones** (*аллофóн*). The decision to see *волнá–вóлны* as (grammatical) variants of a single word has some important consequences for how we understand Russian phonetics. One consequence is that we cannot treat [o] and [ʌ] as we do, say, [п] and [б]. There seems to be a real difference between sounds such as [п] – [б], which are capable of differentiating the meaning of words; whereas the sounds [o] ~ [ʌ] alternate in the *same* word. The sound [ʌ] does not alter the fundamental meaning of words. Though *волнá–вóлны* are variations of a single word (they differ in endings and stress, but not as to fundamental meaning), it is important to note that we are not saying that *вóлны* somehow comes from *волнá*, or vice versa. On the contrary, we suggest that both these words exist independently in the minds of speakers, and that they are related by patterns, one being the akanje rule discussed in 2.3.3.

How can we describe the regular variations of pronunciation (allophones) observed in akanje? Russian speakers regularly identify weak vowels with full vowels because of their positional relationship to stress:

(19)

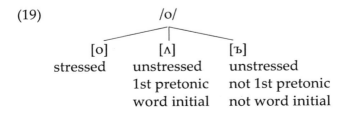

Since the relationships given in (19) are predictable we may call the vowel sounds *predictable variants,* or instances (*инстáнции*), of the category /o/. These instances are simply actually occurring varieties of sounds that are related to each other in word variants. We put all of these sounds into one category and, for purposes of reference, name the category. In this case we name the category "/o/". We could name it anything, but it makes sense to name the category by means of one of the members of the category.

We say /o/ is schematic for [o], [ʌ], and [ъ]. It is important to understand that we are not somehow deriving the instances in (19) from /o/, or from each other. Instead, we are simply stating that as Russians learn to speak they become aware that this relationship exists and they employ this relationship in their own speech. What is the relationship? Simply this:

(20)   [o] when stressed occurs in words in the same place as
       [ʌ] and [ъ], which never occur under stress

Thus Russians know that if you hear an [ʌ], you know it may be related to (i.e., pronounced as) the other two vowel sounds in (20).

We can now set up the first elements of a matrix for akanje:

(21)   /o/   o   ʌ   ъ
       /a/   a   ʌ   ъ

These relationships, however, do not occur randomly. Speakers reading or hearing a new word for the first time are able to pronounce it completely correctly. This is possible because the speaker has internalized generalizations about the distribution of sounds. We represent these generalizations in the matrix:

| (21') | | | C″_–str | |
| | | #_–str, | (exc 1st pretonic | |
	+str	C″_V+str	or initial)	written
/o/	o	ʌ	ъ	*o*
/a/	a	ʌ	ъ	*a*

Practice

A. Given the matrix for akanje above, tell whether or not the following phonetic sequences are found in Russian.

1. [ъкно́]   4. [дава́т’]
2. [лгрлно́м]   5. [о́къл]
3. [малако́]   6. [мъллдо́й]

B. Write the following in phonetic transcription.

1. рисова́ть   6. рыба́лка   11. ошиба́ться
2. ро́дина   7. сиби́рский   12. порошо́к
3. руководя́щий   8. согла́сно   13. похо́жий
4. сморо́дина   9. социоло́гии   14. приближённый
5. смущённо   10. охраня́ть   15. принципиа́льный

C. Read the following out loud. Pay attention to akanje.

О́коло ко́ла колокола́.

Стари́к, уже́ мно́го лет ничего́ не слы́шащий, наконе́ц идёт к врачу́-специали́сту. До́ктор подбира́ет ему́ слуховой аппара́т, и тот сно́ва слы́шит, как в мо́лодости. Спустя́ ме́сяц пацие́нт идёт к врачу́ на консульта́цию.

— Ну что ж, всё в поря́дке. Наверняка́ ва́ша семья́ в восто́рге, что вы сно́ва всё превосхо́дно слы́шите?

— Они́ об э́том ещё не зна́ют. Зато́ я уже́ три́жды переписа́л завеща́ние…

2.4. Other Unstressed Vowels

As is evident from the preceding lesson, stress locus in a Russian word is critical to its proper pronunciation. Stress and phonetics are related in a number of ways. In the previous section we discussed the relationships between the sounds [o], [a], [ʌ], and [ъ]. The distribution of these sounds is limited to stress (the first two), word initial (for the first three), and after a hard consonant (for the last two). Both [o] and [a] (**stressed**) occur after hard consonants and they frequently occur after soft consonants: *упрёк* [упр'о́к], *опять* [лп'а́т']. How about [л] and [ъ]? Do they occur after soft consonants?

2.4.1. Ikanje

The answer to the question asked in the previous section is "no." The reduced sounds [л] and [ъ] never occur after soft consonants. Lebedeva explains:

> В **безударных** позициях после мягких согласных [а, э] ре- дуцируются и приближаются к краткому [и]. В транскрип- ции в первом предударном слоге этот звук обозначается [и]. Например: *весна* [в'исна́], *мясник* [м'исн'и́к]. Во всех других предударных слогах редукция усиливается: здесь произносится очень краткий звук, близкий к [и], но с еще более ослабленной артикуляцией. В транскрипции он обо- значается знаком [ь]. Например: *деловой* [д'ьллвой], *пятачок* [п'ьтлчо́к].

The sound [ь] discussed above is the first vowel sound in English *in- clude*, a very weak high front vowel. According to Lebedeva, un- stressed (written) *я* and *е* are pronounced like [и] (right before the stress) or [ь] in other unstressed positions. Of course when these letters are at the beginning of a word and they are not stressed, they repre- sent [й] followed by the vowel sound (either [и] or [ь], depending on where the stress is):

янва́рь	[йинва́р']
язы́к	[йизы́к]
ерунда́	[йьрунда́]
еди́нственно	[йид'и́нств'ьннъ]

Practice

A. Write the following in normal Russian orthography. Note that for some words more than one written word is possible.

1. [д'э́лъ]
2. [д'ила́]
3. [йида́]

4. [л'эс]
5. [л'иса́]
6. [п'ат']

7. [п'ит'и́]   14. [ка́ф'ьдръ]

8. [ба́бъ йига]   15. [за́йьц]

9. [чьр'ипа́хъ]   16. [д'э́с'ьт']

10. [п'ьр'ьн'ису́]   17. [д'ьс'ит'и́]

11. [вын'ьсу́]   18. [н'имо́й]

12. [д'э́р'ьвъ]   19. [св'ьтлво́й]

13. [р'идъво́й]   20. [пр'имо́й]

B. Prounounce the words above until you feel comfortable with ikanje.

2.4.2. The Ikanje Rule

The relationship between written *я, е* and [и], [ь] can be expressed by a pronunciation rule based on the written letters and the location of stress:

(22)   Ikanje   unstressed *я, е*: [и] v́
                                       [ь] elsewhere

The rule in (22) states that unstressed *я* and *е* are pronounced as [и] when right before the stress. They are pronounced as [ь] everywhere else. Note that this rule also applies to the letter *a* when it falls after a soft consonant: *пятú* [п'ит'и́], *часы́* [чисы́]. Learners can go a long way in improving their pronunciation by paying attention to ikanje.

Practice

A. Write the following in phonetic transcription:

1. чепуха́   6. серебро́

2. телефо́н   7. о́череди

3. берегово́й   8. пятьдеся́т

4. весна́   9. за́нят

5. янва́рь   10. части́ца

B. Read the following out loud. Pay attention to ikanje. Repeat until you can read the text smoothly.

Старик, уже много лет ничего не слышащий, наконец идёт к врачу-специалисту. Доктор подбирает ему слуховой аппарат, и тот снова слышит, как в молодости. Спустя месяц пациент идёт к врачу на консультацию.

—Ну что ж, всё в порядке. Наверняка ваша семья в восторге, что вы снова всё превосходно слышите?

—Они об этом ещё не знают. Зато я уже трижды переписал завещание...

2.4.3. Ikanje and *ё*

So far we have seen that ikanje involves unstressed written *е, я* as [и] [ь], the choice between the latter depending on the location of stress. Ikanje also occurs with "unstressed" *ё*.

Recall that written *ё* represents a soft consonant plus a stressed [o]: *вёл* [в'ол]. When stress is removed, Russians write *е* and the ikanje relation described above works as expected: *вела* [в'ила].

(23) In first pretonic position:

слеза – слёзы	[сл'иза]	[сл'озы]
звезда – звёзды	[зв'изда]	[зв'озды]
черна – чёрный	[чирна]	[чорный]

In other unstressed positions:

слезотечений	[сл'ьзът'ич͡эн'ий]
черновик	[чьрнлв'ик]

Since ikanje affects the pronunciation of all the non-high vowels, we rewrite the ikanje pronunciation rule as follows (compare with (22) in 2.4.2):

(24) Ikanje   unstressed *я, а, е, ё*:   C'[и]v́
                                           C'[ь] elsewhere
                                           (where C'=soft consonant)

The rule in (24) states that the given written letters represent the vowels [и] and [ь] when unstressed **and** when following a soft consonant.

We represent ikanje relationships in a matrix, which depicts orthographic, distributional, and phonetic information:

(25)	+str	C'_V+str	elsewhere	written
/a/	a	и	ь	*а, я*
/э/	э	и	ь	*e*
/o/	o	и	ь	*ё, е*

Native speakers of Russian know the information in (25) in some way. Non-native speakers of Russian whose speech reflects this information have less of an accent than those who do not pay attention to ikanje.

2.4.4. Ykanje

As if that weren't enough, there is one more aspect of unstressed vowel pronunciation that we must review now. Recall that three consonants in Russian are always hard. They are unpaired for softness: [ж], [ш], [ц]. They are always hard, no matter what letter is written after them. Russian spelling rules insist that we never write *я* or *ю* after these consonants, and this makes sense because these letters indicate preceding softness. However, the spelling rules say nothing about written *e*, which freely occurs after **unpaired hard** consonants: *шерсть* [шэрст'], *жёртва* [жэ́ртвъ], *целый* [цэ́лый]. The letter *e* also occurs after unpaired hard consonants when not stressed: *шестой, жена, цена*. Note that ikanje does not apply to these words: though there is a written *e*, it is not preceded by a soft consonant, a critical feature of ikanje. Instead, Russians pronounce [ы]! And in other unstressed positions, Russians pronounce unstressed *e* after unpaired hard consonants as schwa [ъ]! We will call this *ы́канье*. (We might have called it *ъканье*!)

(26)	жена́	[жына́]	жениха́	[жън'иха́]
	цена́	[цына́]	уценена́	[уцън'ина́]

What we have termed ykanje represents an interesting phonetic relationship. It is the only environment in native Russian words in which

[э], written as *e*, occurs after a hard consonant. The ykanje pronunciation rule differs little from our ikanje rule:

(27)   Ykanje   *e*: ж,ш,ц [ы] v́
                       ж,ш,ц [ъ] elsewhere

Practice

A. Write in phonetic transcription:

1. жестóкий	3. шевели́ться
2. шелухá	4. целикóм
5. шестóй	8. кольцевóй
6. желтéть	9. поцелýй
7. жеребёнок	10. шептáть

B. Read the following out loud.

Бáбушка нáша óчень добрá.
Бабýша нáша стáла старá.
Мнóго морщи́нок у бáбушки нáшей
С ни́ми онá ещё лýчше и крáше.

Широкó шагáет Ди́ма,
Он идёт из магази́на.
Ши́ре шаг, ши́ре шаг,
Вот такóй Ди́ма мастáк.

2.4.5. Grammatical Endings

Endings are different. In rapid speech endings are often reduced
greatly or dropped off completely. They convey *grammatical* information such as case, number (singular or plural), and gender. Perhaps
for this reason endings have been treated somewhat differently
throughout the history of Russian and today they are pronounced in
somewhat different ways than what we might expect, given the regularities of akanje and ikanje.

According to ikanje, post-stress *я* is pronounced [ь] as in *месяц* [м'э́с'ьц]. But note that, contrary to ikanje, if the -*я* occurs in an ending it is pronounced [ъ]:

(28) неде́ля   [н'ид'э́л'ъ]
      а́рмия   [а́рм'ийъ]
      зда́ниях   [зда́нийъх]
      но́вая   [но́въйъ]
      чи́стят   [чи́ст'ът]
      занима́ться   [зън'има́цъ]

According to ikanje, post-stress -*е* is pronounced [ь] as in *учи́тель* [учи́т'ьл']. However, if the -*е* occurs in a grammatical ending it is pronounced **either** [ъ] or [ь]. Pronunciation of endings with -*е* as [ъ] is an older, Moscow-type style (and is called the *старомоско́вская но́рма*), but is still very widespread throughout Russia. It occurs in the

nominative singular neuter ending:

| мо́ре | [мо́р'ь] | or | [мо́р'ъ] |
| зда́ние | [зда́н'ийь] | | [зда́н'ийъ] |

instrumental singular masc/neut:

| учи́телем | [учи́т'ьл'ьм] | | [учи́т'ьл'ъм] |
| мо́рем | [мо́р'ьм] | | [мо́р'ъм] |

genitive plural masculine in -ев:

| геро́ев | [г'иро́йьф] | | [г'иро́йъф] |

nominative singular adjective -ое, -ее:

| ста́рое | [ста́ръйь] | | [ста́ръйъ] |

genitive singular masc/neut -его:

| вече́рнего | [в'ичэ́рн'ьвъ] | | [в'ичэ́рн'ъвъ] |

dative singular masc/neut -ему:

| вече́рнему | [в'ичэ́рн'ьму] | | [в'ичэ́рн'ъму] |

simple comparative:

| нове́е | [нлв'э́йь] | | [нлв'э́йъ] |

present tense -ешь, -ет, -ем, -ете:

| чита́ет | [чита́йьт] | | [чита́йът] |

Although the old Moscow norm can be heard, the preferred pronunciation of unstressed -*e* in grammatical endings is [ь]. For the remainder of this text, we will consider the pronunciation of -*e* in grammatical endings as [ь], in other words, as unexceptional. The pronunciation of -*я* as [ъ] in grammatical endings, however, is now the standard pronunciation and we will use that pronunciation throughout this text.

2.4.6. Summary of Ikanje and Ykanje

Ikanje	unstressed *я, а, е, ё*:	C′[и]v́
		C′[ь] elsewhere
Ykanje	unstressed *е*:	ж,ш,ц [ы]v́
		ж,ш,ц [ъ] elsewhere

Practice

A. Write the following in phonetic transcription. Then read each word out loud paying attention to akanje and ikanje.

1. е́хать
2. реда́ктор
3. режиссёр
4. окно́
5. огово́рка
6. погово́рка
7. ребя́та
8. оцени́ть
9. ко́жаный
10. два́дцать
11. огурцы́
12. разреше́ние
13. язы́чный
14. тре́тьего января́
15. пятидесяти́
16. сего́дняшнего
17. челове́к
18. берегово́й
19. серебро́
20. слу́шает

B. Read the following poems out loud.

Мышо́нку ше́пчет мышь:
—Ты всё не спишь, шурши́шь.
Мышо́нок ше́пчет мы́ши:
—Шурша́ть я бу́ду ти́ше.

Ежеви́ку ел ено́т,
Широ́ко рази́нув рот.
Вдруг, из я́годы кула́к,
Показа́л ему́ червя́к.

2.4.7. How to Predict *ё*

When the two dots over *ё* are written, then there is no difficulty in distinguishing it from written *е*: *мёд, место*. However, when the two dots are not written, which is usually the case for Russian, it can be hard to determine if a written *е* represents *ё* or simply *е*. The goal of this section is to determine when stressed *е* is pronounced as *е* and when it is pronounced as *ё*.

From a physiological point of view, it is easy to see why consonants are soft before front vowels ([э], [и]), as in *место* [м'э́стъ]. It's almost as if in preparation of pronouncing the front vowel the preceding consonant is also fronted so that the two are pronounced in a similar way (assimilation). But some consonants are soft before the back vowel [o], as in *нёс* [н'ос]. Consider the following word pairs. A soft consonant followed by [o] can be seen in the second partner of each pair.

(29) легла́   –   лёг
      темно́   –   тёмный
      звезда́   –   звёзды
      несла́   –   нёс
      село́   –   сёла

The data in (29) provide a clue to the distribution of these alternating sounds, namely that *ё* occurs only under stress. However, stress cannot be the only determining factor in the occurrence of *ё*. There are plenty of examples where stressed *е* is not pronounced *ё* [o], such as *зе́лень* or *день*.

Here are some more words that illustrate the alternation of written *е* and *ё*:

(30) ель 'fir tree'   –   ёлка 'fir'
      Пе́тя 'Pete'   –   Пётр 'Peter'
      печь 'to bake'   –   пёк 'he baked'
      пе́рья 'feathers'   –   пёрышко 'little feather'
      пче́льник 'apiary'   –   пчёлы 'bees'

These data suggest that *ё* occurs only before hard consonants. This, too, is assimilation. It's as if in order to prepare for the back tongue position of an upcoming hard consonant, a back consonant [o] is produced instead of the front consonant [э]. We conclude that *e* represents *ё* when it is stressed and precedes a hard consonant. This statement works for many words, but, alas!, there are exceptions, *место*, *лес*, *снег*, for just a few examples (see chapter 7 for the historical reasons behind this). Therefore, our description of when *ё* occurs is really only partially accurate. In fact, it would be more accurate to say that *ё* is **not** pronounced before soft consonants. There are a few exceptions to this formulation as well, but not many, and they are all predictable. The problem with this, however, is that saying what sound a letter does not represent doesn't help with what sound it does represent.

Stress is not normally marked in Russian and it is not always possible to predict whether or not a stressed *e* is *é* or *ё*. As we saw above, stressed *e* usually occurs before a soft consonant, and stressed *ё* before a hard consonant. The following data, however, provide strong counterevidence to this tendency:

(31)	мёд (nom sg)	but	о мёде (prep sg)
	ёлка (nom sg)	but	ёлки (nom pl)
	берёза (nom sg)	but	о берёзе (prep sg)
	живёт (3rd sg)	but	живёте (2nd pl)
	тёмный (long frm)	but	тёмен (short form)
	полёт (nom sg)	but	о полёте (prep sg)

The data in (31) illustrate another aspect of sound patterns. Sometimes they do not occur where it seems they should. This breaking of rules is called analogy (*анало́гия*). For example the sg and pl paradigms for the word *берёза* are given in (32):

(32)	nom	берёза	берёзы
	acc	берёзу	берёзы
	gen	берёзы	берёз
	prep	берёзе ←	берёзах
	dat	берёзе ←	берёзам
	inst	берёзой	берёзами

In all cases of the sg except the prep and dat sg (marked with arrows), and in all cases of the pl the stem of this word ends in a hard consonant. The stem ends in a soft consonant only in the prep/dat sg. **By analogy** to all the other forms of this word, the prep/dat sg forms of this word also keep the stem vowel *ë*. Analogy can be seen at work in the other words given in (30). We will consider analogical forms such as *o мёде* as trivially exceptional insofar as analogy explains their existence.

Practice

A. In the following words stress falls on the underlined vowel. Based on our discussion of the distribution of *é* and *ë*, mark stress on the underlined vowel by using the acute sign ´ or the umlaut sign (two dots) ¨.

1. сельский	6. искривление	11. даете
2. села	7. искривленный	12. веселый
3. звезды (nom pl)	8. истечь	13. веселье
4. ученый	9. истек	14. полет
5. учение	10. шерстка	15. полете

2.5. Assimilation

2.5.1. Final Devoicing

На месте звонких согласных на конце слова произносятся соответстующие глухие.   (Avanesov)

In this quote, the idea of "the end of the word" or "word final position" is important. In phonetic transcription a word boundary is usually transcribed as #. Thus, if a sound falls after the symbol #, it is held to be at the beginning of a word, if it falls before # it is the last sound of the word: [#лкнó#]. In this section we consider the symbol [#] to represent a phonetic reality, the absence of a speech sound.

Avanesov states that voiced consonants are not pronounced at the end of a word. What might be a voiced consonant *in writing* is nevertheless pronounced as its voiceless counterpart in standard Russian. In the following examples pay close attention to the final consonant. Compare its written form to how it is actually pronounced:

(33)	плод	[плот]	сторож	[сто́ръш]
	глаз	[глас]	отре́жь	[лтр'э́ш]
	зуб	[зуп]	сядь	[с'ат']
	нож	[нош]	дом	[дом]
	друг	[друк]	стар	[стар]

As indicated in (33) sonorants are exceptions to the statement offered by Avanesov. We therefore say that just the obstruents (*препятству-ющие*; i.e., all consonants except the sonorants) exhibit this behavior.

The final devoicing rule can be expressed:

(34)   Final Devoicing   C:[–voice]#   (where C=obstruent)

We can get away with calling this assimilation because the boundary of a word can be thought of as a pause or, at least, the absence of any sound, which, in effect, can also be characterized as [–voice]. Final devoicing (*оглуше́ние на конце́ сло́ва*) means that no voiced obstruents are pronounced at the end of a word.

2.5.2. Consonant Clusters

In addition to word final consonants, assimilation affects consonant clusters, when all consonants in the cluster are obstruents: when two or more consonants are next to each other (consonant cluster) then the *VOICED/VOICELESS* characteristic of all of them depends on the voicing nature of the final obstruent in the cluster. Examples:

(35)	тру́бка	[тру́пкъ]	вокза́л	[влгза́л]
	ло́дка	[ло́ткъ]	ска́зка	[ска́скъ]
	вкус	[фкус]	второ́й	[фтлро́й]
	коро́бка	[клро́пкъ]	сгоре́л	[зглр'э́л]
	про́сьба	[про́з'бъ]	изб	[исп]

Taking these data into consideration, we express the assimilation rule:

(36)   Assimilation   C:[±voice] [±voice]   (where C=obstruent)

The pronunciation rule in (36) states that obstruents copy the voicing character of the sound segment to its immediate right.

As indicated by *изб*, the voiceless character of final consonants extends to all obstruents in a word-final cluster. More examples of this:

(37)   визг   'scream'   [в'иск]

       дождь   'rain'   [дошт']

       поезд   'train'   [пойьст]

       борозд   'furrows'   [бʌрóст]

       служб   'services'   [слушп]

       надежд   'hopes'   [нʌд'э́шт]

       дар   'gift'   [дар]

Only obstruents participate in assimilation of voicing characteristics. Sonorants (*л, р, м, н*) play no real role in assimilation. They neither show much the effects of assimilation nor do they trigger assimilation.

What about the letter *в*? It represents an obstruent but in terms of triggering assimilation, it acts like a sonorant.

(38)   <u>assimilates voice</u>   <u>does not trigger assimilation</u>

       вспомнить [фспомн'ит']   свет [св'эт]

       в коридоре [фкър'идóр'ь]   сволочь [сволъч]

2.5.3. Assimilation of Softness

We saw above that when consonants are clustered together they are usually pronounced the same in regard to voice, the final consonant of the cluster determining the voicing character of the preceding consonants. Russians probably do this simply because its easier to pronounce a set of consonants all one way as far as voicing is concerned. How about softness? Is the characteristic of softness also subject to assimilation? Consider the following:

(39) часть [час'т']

вперёд [ф'п'ир'о́т]

дверь [дв'э̂р']

вме́сте [в'м'э̂с'т'ь]

твёрдый [тв'о́рдый]

ски́дка [ски́ткъ]

клева́ть [кл'ива́т']

Softness is assimilated if all the consonants in the cluster have the same PLACE of articulation, i.e., all dentals, all velars, etc. This is particularly important in pronouncing stressed *e* before a soft consonant as [э̂]. Compare the pronunciation, for example, of *присе́л – присе́сть, проте́ст – прочте́сть, сове́т – сове́тница, две – две́сти*.

2.6. Summary of Pronunciation Rules

1. **Tense "e"** 2.2.2

   e: [э̂]C′ (where C′ is a soft consonant)

2. **Yeri** 2.2.3

   и: ж, ш, ц [ы]
   C″[ы] (where C″ is a hard consonant including the
   final consonant of a prefix)

3. **Soft Consonant** 2.2.4

   C′v̈ (where C = any paired consonant and v̈ =
   any front vowel)

4. **Velars** 2.2.5

   K′v̈, Kv̆ (K=velars, v̈=front vowel, v̆=back vowel)

5. **Akanje** 2.3.3

   unstressed *a, o* : #[ʌ], C″[ʌ]Cv́
   : [ъ] elsewhere (where C″ = a hard
   consonant)

6. **Ikanje**   2.4.2, 2.4.6

   unstressed *я, a, e, ё* : C′[и] v́
   : C′[ь] elsewhere

7. **Ykanje**   2.4.4

   unstressed *e* : ж,ш,ц [ы] v́
   : ж,ш,ц [ъ] elsewhere

8. **Assimilation**   2.5.2

   C:[±voice][±voice]   (where C=obstruent and [±voice]≠*в*)

9. **Softness Assimilation**   2.5.3

   C′C′   (where C′=soft consonant and the place of
   articulation for both consonants is the same)

3.1. Derivations

Consider this picture from a Russian book by N. M. Beten'kova that teaches grade-school children how to spell. Why would the spelling of the word for 'river' be a problem for Russian children?

There are numerous ways to express the relationship between stressed *e*, [э], and unstressed *e*, [и]. One way is in the picture at right. Another way, one which is traditionally called the generative approach, asserts that the various pronounced forms of the word for 'river' in Russian can all be derived from one underlying form or base form. For example, in generative phonology, the underlying form of the word *peká* is shown in (1) (where # represents a word boundary).

(1)   # р э к á #

Each segment in this underlying form is a phoneme, an abstract symbol that represents several actual sounds. Of course, the underlying form given above does not occur in normal Russian speech. It is an abstraction, composed of abstract symbols. Rules are then applied to this underlying form to derive the word as it is actually pronounced. In this case, two rules are needed: (i) a rule to soften the /p/ before the front vowel /э/, and (ii) a rule to reduce the vowel /э/ to /и/ (ikanje). The application of rules to an underlying form is called a "derivation." Here are two derivations:

(2) *underlying form*   # р э к á #*NOM.SG*   # р э́ к и #*NOM.PL*

     consonant softening   p'э к á   p'э́ к'и

     ikanje   p'и к á   does not apply

     phonetic   [p'и к á]   [p'э́ к'и]

This is how generative phonology accounts for the relationship between [и] in *реká* and [э] in *réки*. An underlying (abstract) form of a word is set up and all the actually occurring forms of that word are generated from the underlying form.

3.2. Underlying Forms Versus Usage

The generative approach has much to recommend it, not the least being its systematic methodology. We do not wish to discard what is useful about this method, but generative phonology has some important drawbacks. First, the underlying form—such as #рэкá#—does not occur in Russian in any word. Paired consonants are always soft before front vowels, and we know that the sound [э] can occur only under stress. Therefore the proposed underlying form does not exist in reality. Generativists answer that the underlying form is a handy abstraction that generates, with proper rules, all forms that do exist. Our point is that as an abstraction it represents no actually occurring form.

In a usage-based approach, such as the one presented in this text, variants such as [p'икá] and [p'э́к'и] are learned by experience and exist side by side in the speaker's mind. There is no need to generate either one. The speaker can choose whichever one is needed in a given context. Generalizations (i.e., rules) which relate alternations emerge in a speaker's mind based on actual linguistic input, i.e., based on what the speaker actually says and hears every day. In a usage-based program, the structure of the language is overt, it is not derived from a deeper (unverifiable) abstraction. It therefore seems reasonable to assert that a usage based description, such as the one presented in this text, renders a better picture of reality than the generative-based description.

3.3. Schemas

Throughout this text we use a simple tool, the schema, to describe relationships between specific linguistic tokens and the meaningful categories to which they belong. For the various forms of the word *река́*, for example, we write the schema:

(3)

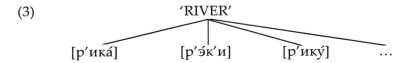

(The three dots above indicate there are other forms that could fit in here, too. We're just not bothering to list all the forms of this word.)

Note that in this schema only actually-occurring forms are part of the description. When children learning Russian first hear these words (in any case form) they store them away in memory as pronounced, having learned what their referent is. Later they misspell the word in school, assuming that *и* stands for all instances of [и], because they have heard [p'ика́] (or another singular form) much more often than the plural [p'э́к'и]. (Shteinfeldt reports this word is used 84% in the singular, 16% in the plural.)

The second reason why we find the generative approach untenable is that it implies that whenever speakers want to use, say, the genitive form of the word, they **apply one or more phonological rules to an abstraction** to come up with the proper pronunciation. We think this is unlikely. Even more unlikely is the flip side of that coin. If speakers hear [p'ик'а́], they must apply some rule to degenerate this word to its **basic** abstract form [рэка́]. The problem with this is that, as discussed in chapter two, phonetic [и] may be associated with /э/, /и/, /a/, or /o/! No generative rule could pick the proper association without looking at other forms of the word, which would essentially make it a usage-based approach.

In cognitive grammar we deal with "abstractions" (such as phonemes /a/, /o/, /т/, etc.), but only as names of categories of sounds. Thus the phoneme /a/ is an abstraction in that it represents all the possible pronunciations of a low back vowel in Russian, but it also represents the pronunciation of [a], a low back vowel. The same is true with meaning. The "abstraction" /RIVER/ refers to whatever rivers the speaker knows about and may even represent a prototypical river, but it also relates to the Volga or some other specific actually occurring river. The abstraction is nothing more than a useful category name that comes from the actually encountered instances.

(4)

Where the category name is one of the instances and stands for the rest.

Why is any of this important? Aren't we straying quite far from the goal of practicing Russian sounds to improve our ability to speak Russian? Yes and no. Yes, we have been discussing some fairly theoretical aspects of this presentation. But the concepts presented here are useful for understanding the relationships between sounds and words in Russian. By understanding these concepts, we better understand their relationships and so are better able to describe Russian pronunciation, which otherwise might seem to be just a chaotic jumble of mutations, alternations, stress shifts, and disconnects between pronunciation and spelling. In addition, understanding the theoretical framework used here to describe phonology helps provide a foundation for understanding the concepts introduced in the rest of this book.

Consider the following words and their pronunciation:

(5) мя́со [м'а́съ]   мясни́к [м'исн'и́к]   мясника́ [м'ьсн'ика́]
     'meat'   'butcher'   'butcher' (gen sg)

In these semantically related words we observe the following alternations in the root of each:

(6) [a] ~ [и] ~ [ь]

Though we observe three variations in these related roots, we want to avoid questions like, "In the root meaning 'butcher' what vowel sound is it really? Which one of the three variants is basic? What rules derive the others from the basic sound?" We answer these questions:

There are three sounds here. None is more basic than any other. So...

None is derived from any other.

But **there is an important relationship** between these sounds. It is important because it occurs throughout the language. We definitely want to account for (describe) this relationship. We do this by means of different kinds of schemas.

A **schema** can simply represent an observed relationship between sounds:

(7)

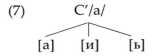

Literate speakers connect written symbols with spoken ones. We can also capture this reality with a **schema**:

(8)

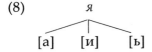

There are other types of schemas that we will use in later chapters. All the information we have about phonetic relationships can be combined into a single matrix:

(9)		+str	pretonic; C′__	−str; C′__	written
	/a/	[a]	[и]	[ь]	я

Speakers of contemporary standard Russian have intuited this information. When they want to refer to /BUTCHER/, they choose a string of sounds that they have heard and which represents this sense. They say [м′исн′и́к]. When they use this word in the accusative case, they choose [м′ьсн′ика́]. They know these are instances of a single lexical item because the sense matches and because the schematic given above **authorizes** or **validates** the alternation in pronunciation. Authorization is a concept which simply states that a speaker has

searched for and found sensible (compatible) stored information that
matches what is being spoken or heard. In the case of [м′исн′и́к] and
[м′ьсн′ика́] the match is perfect.

When speakers hear these words, they judge what sounds they are
hearing and search for the matching sounds that most closely correspond to what they have heard. When found, a reference to some aspect of the meaning of the word within the context of the utterance is
made. Speakers may also say something unauthorized by the matrix,
[м′асн′ика́], for example. This pronunciation may still be understood
by a native speaker because it is still partially authorized by the matrix
(horizontally) though not fully authorized (both horizontally and
vertically).

Practice

A. Which of the phonetic sequences below are fully authorized by the
matrix in (9). Which ones are partially authorized, and which ones
are not authorized at all?

1. синя́к	[с′ин′а́к]
2. синяка́	[с′ин′ика́]
3. синя́к	[с′ин′о́к]
4. синяка́	[с′ин′ака́]
5. синяка́	[с′ин′ька́]

3.4. и and ы

We now ask about the relationship between the two sounds [и] and
[ы]. We know they are in complementary distribution: [и] occurs only
after soft consonants and in word initial position, and [ы] occurs only
after hard consonants. This suggests there is only one category, /и/,
and within this category are the two sounds [и] and [ы]:

(10)   C″__   C′__   written

      /и/   [ы]   [и]   ???

In this case the writing system allows two written forms *ы* and *и* as representing /и/. This is not too bad, because an ambiguity in the spelling of [ы] already occurs in modern Russian:

(11)   [игра́т'] *игра́ть* 'play'   [сыгра́т'] *сыгра́ть* 'play (pf.)'

We choose /и/ to represent this category for two reasons. First, of the two only [и] occurs in nature independently: at word initial position and by itself in the word *и* 'and'. Second, written *и* sometimes represents [ы] in the modern Russian alphabet. Recall that one part of the Yeri rule (section 2.2.3) specifies that written *и* is pronounced [ы] after the hushers *ш*, *ж* and after *ц*, as in *жить* [жыт']. The second part of that rule states that after prefixes *и* is pronounced (and written) as [ы] as in *игра́ть* ~ *сыгра́ть*.

Important note: the existence of the Yeri rule does not imply that the sound [ы] exists **only** in connection with written *и*. For example, in *столы́* 'tables', the nom pl ending has no connection with *и*.

Practice

A. Given the matrix above, explain whether or not the following are authorized in Russian.

1. [бы́л]	11. [йизы́к]
2. [б'ы́л]	12. [ты́л]
3. [жы́л]	13. [кри́шкъ]
4. [жи́л]	14. *ды́рка*
5. [ысп'и́т']	15. *улы́бчывый*
6. [йы́сл'и]	16. *цикло́н*
7. [учи́т']	17. *цы́почка*
8. [цы́рк]	18. *раду́шие*
9. [и́ст'инъ]	19. *шы́ворот*
10. [п'ьр'э́д'н'ый]	20. *жыво́й*

3.5. Review

Once after playing a particularly difficult étude, the great pianist Robert Schumann was asked to explain the piece. In response, he sat down and played the piece again.

This review is in the spirit of Robert Schumann.

A. Read the following out loud.

> Же́нщина купа́ется в реке́,
> Со́лнце замира́ет вдалеке́,
> Не́жно положи́в на пле́чи ей
> Руки́ золоты́х свои́х луче́й.
> Ря́дом с ней, каса́ясь головы́,
> Мо́кнет тень берегово́й листвы́.
> Затиха́ют травы́ на лугу́,
> Ка́мени мо́крые на берегу́,
> Пле́щется купа́льщица в воде́,
> Не́ту зла, и сме́рти нет нигде́.
> В ми́ре нет ни вью́ги, ни зимы́,
> Нет тюрьмы́ на све́те, ни сумы́.
> Войн ни на одно́м материке́...
> Же́нщина купа́ется в реке́.
>   (К. Кули́ев, 1964)

B. Be ready to answer the following questions orally.

1. Что лу́чше: бо́льше ма́леньких кани́кул во вре́мя уче́бного го́да и́ли бо́лее дли́нные ле́тние кани́кулы?

2. Обяза́тельно ли ну́жно принести́ пода́рок, когда́ идёшь в го́сти?

3. Есть ли больша́я по́льза в уче́нии како́му-нибу́дь музыка́льному инструме́нту?

4. Как лу́чше пра́здновать день рожде́ния?

5. Должны́ ли де́ти носи́ть шко́льную фо́рму?

6. В како́м шта́те вы хоте́ли бы жить? Почему́?

7. Во ско́лько у нас в Аме́рике де́ти стано́вятся совершенноле́тними. Чего́ э́то каса́ется?

8. Ско́лько раз в неде́лю должны́ ли мы у́жинать до́ма?

9. Как вы отно́ситесь к введе́нию де́тского коменда́тского ча́са?

10. Сто́ит ли, по ва́шему, постро́ить ба́зу на луне́?

Part II

Russian Morphology and Morphophonemics

It's one thing to speak Russian well, another to understand how Russian is put together and how to make sense of the manifold irregularities that plague both native speakers and learners of Russian. Anyone with an expertise in Russian should have at least a basic idea of how to account for its inflectional irregularities, alternations in derivation, spelling conventions, fleeting vowels, and other important aspects of the language. Earlier we discussed how Russian sounds interact with each other in words and we presented a means for describing this interaction. The following chapters will introduce a description of how Russian words are put together by means of roots, suffixes, and endings.

Keep in mind that the goal of these chapters is to **describe** how Russian words are put together. We want to do so in a consistent and straightforward way and, during the process, we want to capture as many generalizations as possible about the modern language. The approach taken, therefore, is a *synchronic* account of Russian word formation: we limit our investigation strictly to the language that is used by speakers today. We hope that this methodology mimics in some way the knowledge that native speakers of Russian gain about their language. The main questions we want to answer are:

(1) What are the component parts of Russian words?

(2) What happens when these components are combined?

(3) How does our description simplify apparent irregularities in declension and conjugation?

(4) What processes characterize word formation?

A description of a language does not answer why a language is the way it is. It simply is a description of a current state. To answer "why," we must look at the historical development of the language: what happened hundreds and thousands of years ago that made the language as it appears today. That would be a *diachronic* description and will be the task of Part III. However, before we attempt to understand the "why," it is important first to understand the "what."

4.1. Introduction

Russian words are composed of units of sound. A morpheme (*морфéма*) is a sequence of sounds (or the absence of sound) that has some kind of lexical meaning. For example, in the word *председáтель*, we can see several morphemes: the prefix *пред-* meaning 'in front of,' the root *сед-* 'to sit,' and the suffix *-атель* 'an agent.' When this word is declined, such as in the gen sg *председáтеля*, the ending *-я* is a morpheme which expresses a grammatical relationship, such as "possession." In addition, a complete word can be composed of a single morpheme: *стол* 'table.'

"Inflectional morphology" (*морфолóгия* or more specifically *словоизменéние*) refers to the process of adding endings to word stems. "Inflectional" means "having to do with endings." "Morphology" means "the science of forming." Inflectional morphology shows the order and simplicity (as far as these exist) in the system of endings used in Russian, and is therefore a valuable topic of study for students of Russian. Through inflectional morphology we open up words to discover their composition.

4.2. The Spelling Rule *o* ~ *e*

An important spelling rule of Russian pertains to the hushers, also known as palatal consonants: *ш, ч, щ, ж* and to the affricate *ц*. The spelling rule involving these letters is often expressed:

(1)   Unstressed *o* alternates with *e* after hushers and *ц*.

The instr sg masc noun endings provide good examples of this spelling rule:

(2) журн**а́**л**ом**

    каранд**а**ш**о́м**   but   д**у́**ш**ем**

    отц**о́м**   м**е́**сяц**ем**

Are there two endings, -*ом* and -*ем*, or just two variants of a single ending, -*ом*? The following facts suggest that we are dealing with two variants of a single ending. First, the two inst sg masc noun endings (written -*ом* and -*ем*) share a number of characteristics, namely **case** (instrumental), **number** (singular), **gender** (both are masculine), and even **phonetic form** (both have the structure *mid vowel + м*). They also share the same meaning. Secondly, these two forms are in **complementary distribution** (*дополни́тельное распределе́ние*), which means that one always occurs in one environment (next to a hard paired consonant) and the other in a different environment (next to a husher or *ц*). This suggests that, in addition to stress, it is the environment that is important in determining which variant is used, namely the environment specified in (1). This spelling rule explains many alternations. In endings and suffixes, *o* will alternate with *e* when it is not stressed and follows a husher or *ц*. We represent this with the following schema, the actual (written) occurrences are related to each other via a morpheme (in curly brackets):

(3)   {+ом}

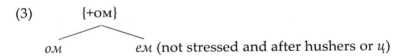

    ом   *ем* (not stressed and after hushers or *ц*)

    Beginning students of Russian often forget the rule in (1) or confuse it with other rules. This is understandable. The rule seems totally capricious. We will see later that the rule actually makes a lot of sense. However, just looking at the modern language and how words with the letter -*o* in them behave, we see that the phenomenon of -*o* alternating with -*e* occurs in positions beyond what the spelling rule in (1) predicts. For example, consider the following:

(4) журн**а́**л**ом** (instr sg)   ending -*ом*   but уч**и́**тел**ем** (instr sg)

      н**о́**в**ое** (nom neut)   ending -*oe*   but веч**е́**рн**ее** (nom neut)

By expanding the spelling rule in (1) to include the environment of **any soft consonant**, we can account for the differences in spelling (and pronunciation) evident in the endings in (4):

(5)   Unstressed *o* alternates with *e* after hushers, *ц*, and **any soft consonant.**

The generalization in (5) is a synchronic description in regard to the relationship between the letters -*o* and -*e*. It makes no reference to history or **why** things are this way, and it does not imply the one form (-*ем*) is derived from or comes from the other (-*ом*). The two forms are simply related. They both exist in reality and all we are doing is relating them in a formal way. Incidental to the rule in (5) is the implication that when unstressed the letter *o* occurs only after hard consonants. In Russian, unstressed -*o* after a soft consonant does not occur. Instead, we find -*e*. Similarly, the letter -*e* does not occur after hard consonants (except *ш*, *ж*, and *ц*). We will see that the rule in (5) reveals much about the seemingly exceptional forms in Russian declension and conjugation.

Practice

A. How should the schema in (3) be changed to reflect the information in (5)?

B. Try writing an unstressed -*o*- after a soft consonant.

C. In the following words, the *e* in each word is related to an *o* through the spelling rule. For each word given, think of a Russian word that shows the same ending only with an -*o*. For example: хоро́ш<u>его</u> → но́в<u>ого</u>

хоро́ш<u>ему</u>	това́рищ<u>ем</u>	хоро́ш<u>ей</u>
ме́сяц<u>ев</u>	учи́тельниц<u>ей</u>	строи́тел<u>ем</u>

4.3. Masculine Nouns

You know the basic facts about Russian nouns—case, number, and gender. In addition, you know spelling rules that account for differences in some endings, e.g., inst sg masc стол<u>о́м</u> but ме́сяц<u>ем</u>. We have seen that this rule really is just the tip of a much more general rule, one whose operation will uncover much of the orderliness of the inflectional system.

In a sense, this spelling rule allows us to limit the number of endings that occurs in the noun system. Thus, instead of saying there are two inst sg masc endings *-ом* and *-ем*, we can say there is just one morpheme, namely {+ом} and that *-ом* and *-ем* are variants of each other. Their relationship is described in 4.2 (5).

The masc sg noun endings are given in (6). In this chart there are three sets of endings. Each set corresponds to the three traditional nom sg masc endings: # (consonant), ь (soft sign), and *й*.

(6) nom	#	ь	й	(стол	учи́тель	музе́й)
acc	↕	↕	↕			
gen	а	я	я			
prep	е	е	е*			
dat	у	ю	ю			
inst	ом	ем**	ем**			

    * -и if the noun ends in -ий
    ** -ём when stressed

The chart in (6) has eighteen endings. Inflectional morphology lets us see in these endings just five **morphemes**. The other 13 endings are simply variations.

First we eliminate the acc endings since they are identical to the nom and gen endings: acc inanimate = nom, acc animate = gen. As shown in (6), there is no unique ending for masc nouns in the accusative.

It looks like there are three endings for the nom sg: consonant (#), ь, and *й*. It is only the alphabetic letters, however, that make it appear this way. Recall that *-й-* is a consonant and that *-ь-* only occurs with consonants. In fact, the nom sg masc endings all end in a consonant; examples: *стол* (л is a hard consonant), *учи́тель* (ль is a soft consonant), *музе́й* (й is a soft consonant). All other cases are marked by a vowel ending. The nom, however, just ends in any consonant. It has no vowel ending. We see that there are not three nom sg masc endings (#, ь, and *й*), but one, namely the "no ending" or "zero ending," the lack of an overt ending.

We use **morphological transcription** to indicate how Russian words are put together by morphemes. In morphological transcription "zero ending" is transcribed as a Ø. The term +Ø implies that there is an ending (indicated by +) but that the ending is empty, there is no vocalic ending. In Russian the absence of an overt vocalic ending, however, counts as a case marker. Morphological transcriptions of words illustrating this are given in (7).

(7) стол {стол +Ø}   учитель {учитэл' +Ø}   музей {музэй +Ø}

Note that **morphological** transcription is written in curly brackets. While each of these words ends in a different sound, they all end in a consonant and they all share the same nom sg ending, namely {+Ø}.

Morphological transcriptions (MT) are written in curly brackets so as not to confuse them with phonetic transcription, e.g., [учит'ъл']. In addition, endings are marked by a plus sign ({стол +óм}). An equals sign is used to show the presence of a prefix: {про=хóд +Ø}. Paired soft consonants are marked by an apostrophe when softness is not automatic. Stress is always marked in MT. Note that only the vowel letters *o, u, y, ы, a,* and *э* are ever used in MT.

The difference between hard and soft consonants in Russian is fundamental and it is always indicated in writing. This is done by means of the hard and soft signs, and by the extraordinary device of having two sets of vowel letters for each vowel sound. One vowel letter indicates that the preceding consonant is hard, its partner—soft. For example, in *мать* 'mother' the *м* is shown to be hard because the vowel letter *a* follows it. However, in *мять* 'crumple' the *м* is shown to be soft because the vowel letter *я* follows it.

While the orthography (regular writing) shows these differences by different vowel letters, MT is more consistent in its transcriptions, in that one vowel sound is always represented the same way. If softness is automatic (as with *-ч-, -й-,* and *-щ-* and paired consonants before *-e-* and *-u-*) then no apostrophe is written in MT, since softness in these consonants is predictable. In words where a soft paired consonant precedes a back vowel, *-a-, -o-, -y-* or at the end of a word, then softness is not predictable and so must be written in MT: {мат' +Ø}, {м'ат' +Ø}.

The relationships between morphological transcription and written vowel letters are presented in the following chart (where *m'* stands for a soft consonant, and *m* stands for any hard consonant).

(8) Й + Vowel		Soft Consonant + Vowel		Hard Consonant + Vowel	
MT	orth.	MT	orth.	MT	orth.
{йа}	я	{т'а}	тя	{та}	та
{йо}	ё / е[1]	{т'о}	тё / те[2]	{то}	то
{йу}	ю	{т'у}	тю	{ту}	ту
{йэ}	е	{т'э}	те	{тэ}	те[3]
{йи}	и	{т'и}	ти	{ти}	ти[3]
{йы}	и	{т'ы}	ти	{ты}	ты[4]

Notes:

1. When stressed {й + ó} is represented by orthographic -*ё*, without stress it is -*е*.
2. When stressed {т' + ó} is represented by orthographic -*тё*. Without stress, it is -*те*.
3. A hard consonant followed by a front vowel {э} or {и} is pronounced soft (by rule—discussed below). This combination is represented by orthographic -*те* and -*ти*.
4. Note that {ы} is spelled as *и* after *к, г, х* by rule (discussion below).

The orthographic device illustrated in (8) accounts for the variations observed in the gen sg masc endings, where there is simply one morpheme, namely {+a}. Examples are in morphological transcription:

(9) morphological: {стол +á}   {учи́тэл' +a}   {музэ́й +a}
     orthographic: стола́   учи́теля   музе́я

We conclude that the two variations for gen sg masc, -*a* and -*я*, can be represented by the single morpheme {+a}.

Practice

A. What are the prep, dat, and inst masc sg endings in morphological transcription? Give an example of each in MT. Be sure to write out each word in normal Russian, as well (as in (9)).

B. Write out the following in normal (orthographic) transcription:

1. {д'а́д' + а}   4. {муж + Ø}   7. {богач + о́м}

2. {учи́тэл' + у}   5. {му́ж + ом}   8. {царэ́вич + ом}

3. {мэ́с'ац + э}   6. {м'од + Ø}   9. {вэк + а́}

C. Write out the following in morphological transcription:

1. бе́рег   4. ле́бедю   7. студе́нта   10. геро́ем

2. ле́бедь   5. зу́бе   8. профи́ля

3. мудрецо́м   6. словарём   9. геро́я

4.4. Two Other "Spelling Rules"

As discussed earlier, the front vowels *e* and *u* are special in that they are preceded by soft consonants (see section 2.2.4). Earlier we represented this as the phonetic relationship C'v̈, in which paired consonants are soft before front vowels. Now that we are investigating inflectional morphology, we can see that this helps to explain a predictable alternation that occurs when we add a morpheme beginning with an {э} or {и}. This alternation can be represented in a schema (where C refers to any paired consonant—a consonant that can be hard or soft—and C' refers to any soft consonant):

(10)

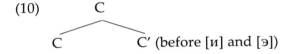

Thus, the prep sg masc ending {э} follows a soft consonant, even if the consonant is not soft in other cases. Consider, for example, the word *гриб* 'mushroom.' In many of its cases the stem ends in a hard consonant. But elsewhere the final consonant is soft, as in the prep sg:

(11)   MT: {гриб + э́}   phon. [гр'иб'э́]   ortho.   *грибе́*

Note that only the phonetic and orthographic forms represent actually occurring language. The MT is simply a handy way of describing the component morphemes of any given word. Since paired consonants are soft before front vowels, we do not need to indicate soft-ness in the MT of this word. MT shows what is not predictable. For example, the first letter for the word meaning 'mushroom' could be just about any consonant. There's no way to predict that it is a *z*; it could just as easily be a *б* or a *m*. We include in MT only idiosyncratic, nonpredictable information. Since the softness of the *б* **is** predictable in (11), we don't include it in MT. We are interested in MT because it al-lows us to capture generalizations that otherwise would be invisible.

Now consider the alphabetic letters -*ы* and -*и*. They occur in the following situations:

(12) **in writing**

	ы	и
after hard consonants	yes	no
after soft consonants	no	yes
after hushers	no	yes
after к, г, х	no	yes

This suggests that a rule exists that relates these two letters. The "spelling rule" is traditionally stated (compare with the Yeri rule in 2.2.3):

(13) Don't write -*ы*- after hushers or gutturals (к, г, х), instead write -*и*-.

As we can see by comparing (12) and (13), the traditional spelling rule does not completely capture the relationship between *ы* and *и*. The written letter -*ы*- also never occurs after soft consonants. We can express this state of affairs with a schema, where Č refers to any husher and K refers to к, г, or х:

(14)   {+ы}

ы   *и* (after C', Č, K)

The schema in (14) states that the morpheme {+ы} is spelled as *и* in the environments mentioned. (For pronunciation, the situation is slightly different. We know from the Yeri pronunciation rule that written *ы* is always pronounced [ы] and that written *и* is pronounced [ы] after ж, ш, and ц.) The existence of this rule will allow us to simplify our description of Russian morphology. For example, it shows that the nom pl morpheme ending for masc nouns {+ы} can represent the ending in forms such as *писа́тели*. But more about plural forms later.

4.5. Declension Class Versus Gender

It is common for learners of Russian to designate types of endings by referring to gender, such as "masculine." Another designation is to declension (decl) class (*склоне́ние*), such as 1st decl class, 2nd decl class, etc. Reference to declension class is more precise than "masculine" because there are masc nouns that take different endings, such as *де́душка* and *доми́шко*. These latter belong to the 2nd and 4th decl classes, respectively. Thus 1st declension nouns are masculine nouns that end in a consonant in the nom sg, while 2nd decl nouns end in the vowel {+a} in the nom sg, 3rd decl nouns are fem nouns ending in zero in the nom sg (for example, *ночь*) and neut nouns in *-мя*. Finally, 4th decl nouns take the vowel {+o} in the nom sg.

Two other endings not discussed above are the so-called "loc2" and "gen2" endings. The loc2 ending {+ý} is used only in certain monosyllabic 1st decl nouns after the prepositions *в* or *на*: *в лесу́, на мосту́*. The gen2 ending is {+y}, normally used with certain 1st decl nouns indicating a partitive notion: *ча́ю, шокола́ду, са́хару*; "some tea," etc. See chapter 7 for the historical background of these endings.

Practice

A. In 4.3 (6) we listed 18 endings for masc sg nouns. Write out the **five** morphemes that represent these endings. These are the inflectional morphemes for 1st decl sg nouns.

B. Write the following in MT in nom, gen, prep, dat, and inst sg.

    1. го́род   2. разбо́й   3. календа́рь (end stress)

4.6. Second Declension

Fem sg noun endings (or better, 2nd decl sg endings—not all nouns taking these endings are fem) are listed in their orthographic form in (15).

(15)	nom	а	я	ия
	acc	у	ю	ию
	gen	ы	и	ии
	prep	е	е	ии
	dat	е	е	ии
	inst	ой	ей	ией

Examples for the nom case are given in (16):

(16) газе́та   неде́ля   аллерги́я

Practice

A. Using the generalizations in 4.3 (8) regarding the morphological representation of *я*, tell what morpheme represents the 2nd decl nom sg endings.

B. Write out the three words in (16) in morphological transcription.

C. Write out the acc sg, gen sg, and inst sg morphemes.

D. Which two cases in 2nd decl have identical endings?

Note that the prep and dat case ending has two forms: -*e* and -*u* (as in *в а́рмии*). We will consider this ending the same as that for the gen -*uu* and dat. -*uu*.

Recall that *ы* is never written after velars, hushers, or soft consonants; instead we write *и*. Since this state of affairs exists, we are able to propose a single morpheme for the gen sg, namely {+ы}. The morphological transcription of the gen sg *боги́ни* can be expressed as: {боги́н′ + ы}.

Similarly, the inst sg endings *-ой, -ей* can be represented by a single morphological ending, namely, {+ой}.

(17) inst sg fem orthrographic *неде́лей*

MT {нэдэ́л′ + ой} morpheme is {-ой} — compare with *газе́той*

When stress falls on the ending of a 2nd decl noun whose stem ends in a soft consonant the *o* of the instr morpheme {+ой} can be heard:

(18) inst sg fem orthographic *земле́й*

MT {зэмл′ +о́й}

In *земле́й*, the letter *ё* is used in place of *o* to show the preceding consonant is soft.

Practice

E. Write in normal orthography the following words given in MT and tell which case ending is being used.

1. {доли́н + а}   4. {ба́шн′ + а}   7. {стат′й + а́}
2. {доли́н + ой}   5. {ба́шн′ + ой}   8. {стат′й + о́й}
3. {доли́н + ы}   6. {ба́шн′ + ы}   9. {стат′й + э́}

F. Write the following words in morphological transcription.

1. ли́ния (nom sg)   7. пе́сня (nom sg)
2. ли́нии (gen sg)   8. пе́сни (gen sg)
3. кни́ги (gen sg)   9. пе́сней (inst sg)
4. семью́ (acc sg)   10. пе́сню (acc sg)
5. ступнёй (inst sg)   11. ку́хне (dat sg)
6. ли́нией (inst sg)   12. ли́нию (acc sg)

4.7. Third and Fourth Declensions

The 3rd decl class is composed mostly of fem nouns that end in a soft sign (stems end in a soft consonant followed by the zero morpheme), e.g., *дверь, лошадь, ночь*. Also belonging to this class is the single masc noun *путь* 'path' and the ten neut nouns ending *-мя* (*время, имя*, etc.). Here are the endings in both orthographic and morphological representation, as illustrated by the paradigm of *лошадь*.

(19) nom   лошадь   {лошад' + Ø}

acc   лошадь   {лошад' + Ø}

gen   лошади   {лошад' + и}

prp   лошади   {лошад' + и}

dat   лошади   {лошад' + и}

inst лошадью   {лошад' + йу}

Since all stems in the 3rd decl end in a soft consonant it might be suggested that the ending for the gen sg is {+ы} (as in 2nd declension), which would be realized as *-u* according to spelling rule. We have chosen the morpheme {+и}, however, because this is the historically correct ending (see section 7.6) and it shows the common identity of endings in this declension (gen=prep=dat). It is also important to note that, unlike 2nd decl, there is no alternation between *ы* and *и* in 3rd decl. The only ending we find in gen sg of 3rd decl is *и*.

Notice in (19) that the soft sign disappears after the nom/acc but then reappears again in the inst. Since there is no ending in the nom/acc, we show the word ends in a soft consonant by a soft sign. The letter *-и* serves this purpose for the gen, prep, and dat cases. So, why does the soft sign suddenly pop up again in the inst sg? Why is it needed? After all the letter *-ю-* indicates that preceding consonants are soft.

The answer to this question, oddly enough, is that the *-ь* shows the presence of the i-kratkoe in the ending {+йу}. Compare the following forms:

(20) a. MT   {лошад' + у}

orth   *лошадю

(20) b. MT   {ло́шад' + йу}
          orth   ло́шадью

The form in (20a) does not exist. But it shows how the word in question would look **if the ending were simply {+у}**. However, the ending is {+йу}, as shown in (20b). In this situation, we see that when a soft consonant is followed by an i-kratkoe, the consonant is written with a soft sign and the i-kratkoe is represented by one of the vowel letters *-ю, -я, -ё, -и, -е* (section 1.1.2). Here are two more examples: *семья́* {сэм'й +а́}, *питьё* {пит'й + о́}. The soft sign is written both to indicate preceding softness and to indicate the presence of an i-kratkoe.

The 4th decl is made up primarily of neut nouns. Here are the endings as they occur orthographically.

(21)

nom	o	e	ие
acc	o	e	ие
gen	a	я	ия
prp	e	e	ии
dat	y	ю	ию
ins	ом	ем	ием

Examples of words that take these endings are: *ме́сто, по́ле*, and *зда́ние*. For the most part the endings of the 4th decl are identical to those of the 1st decl: gen {+a}, prep {+э}, dat {+у}, inst {+ом}, and 2nd decl (prep {+и} following *ий*). But the nom/acc endings deserve some scrutiny.

The orthography makes it appear that we are dealing with three endings: *-o, -e*, and *-ие*. But if we appeal to the *o ~ e* spelling rule we can see that there is only one nom sg neut morpheme, namely {+o}. When not stressed and following a soft consonant or a husher, this ending is realized orthographically as *-e*:

(22)

orthographic	ме́сто	по́ле	зда́ние
morphological	{мэ́ст + o}	{по́л' + o}	{зда́ний + o}

We can verify the assertion that {+o} is the morpheme for the neut nom with stems ending in a soft consonant by finding words with final stress, such as *окно́* and *питьё*. In these words we hear the [o] sound of the ending.

Practice

A. Write the following words in morphological transcription and indicate what case they are in.

1. питьё
2. дочь
3. любо́вь
4. питья́
5. пло́щади
6. свинья́
7. ко́мнаты
8. дверь
9. ло́шадью
10. го́ре
11. учи́телю
12. две́рью

B. Words whose nom sg ends in a soft sign followed by *-я*, *-е*, or *-ё*
(e.g., *судья́*, *статья́*, *сва́тья*, *бельё*, *чиха́нье*) have an {й} in the
stem: {суд'**й** + а́}, for example. Why doesn't the soft sign disappear
orthographically in **any** case of the sg of these words?

C. What do the inst sg morphemes for 2nd declension and 3rd declension have in common? Consider the following sentence from
Tolstoy's *War and Peace*:

Де́тскость выраже́ния её лица́ в соедине́нии с то́нкой
красото́ю ста́на составля́ли её осо́бенную пре́лесть,
кото́рую он хорошо́ по́мнил.

What's going on with the inst sg ending in the word красото́ю?

D. Nouns ending in *-ие* and *-ия* in the nom conceal an {й} as in
чте́ние {чт'э́ний + о}. In what case in the pl of these nouns does
the {-й} become visible in the normal orthography?

4.8. Plural Endings

Differences between declension classes in the pl occur only in the nom
and gen cases. There are no independent acc pl endings: for animate
nouns the acc pl matches the gen pl, for inanimates the acc pl is the
same as nom pl. And this is true of all declensions. The prep case mor-

pheme is {+ах} for all declensions, dat has {+ам}, and inst takes {+ами} for all declensions. Differences between declensions occur partly in the nom pl and to the greatest degree in the gen pl. We will discuss the nom pl first.

As indicated in (23) below, the 1st, 2nd, and 3rd decl nom pl orthographic ending is either *ы* or *и*. For 1st and 2nd decl, we can say that the morpheme representing these endings is {+ы}, recalling that *ы* is written *и* after hushers, velars, and soft consonants.

(23)		1st Decl	2nd Decl	3rd Decl	4th Decl
nom sg		Ø ь й	а я ия	ь	о е ие
nom pl		ы и и	ы и ии	и	а я ия
acc pl		↕	↕	↕	↕
gen pl		ов ей ев	Ø ь ий	ей	Ø ей ий
prep pl		ах ях ях	ах ях иях	ях	ах ях иях
dat pl		ам ям ям	ам ям иям	ям	ам ям иям
inst pl		ами ями ями	ами ями иями	ями	ами ями иями

The nom pl morpheme for 3rd decl nouns could also be {+ы} (since all 3rd decl nouns end in a soft consonant). However, this declension has the ending -*и* throughout the sg, and since the historical nom pl ending -*и* for this declension never alternates with -*ы*, we suggest the nom pl morpheme for 3rd decl nouns is {+и}.

There is only one nom pl morpheme for 4th decl nouns, namely {+a}.

(24)	1st Decl	2nd Decl	3rd Decl
	заво́ды {заво́д+ы}	ка́рты {ка́рт+ы}	тетра́ди {тетра́д'+и}
	мучи́тели {мучи́тэл'+ы}	неде́ли {нэдэ́л'+ы}	
	геро́и {гэро́й+ы}	а́рмии {а́рмий+ы}	

Practice

A. Write in morphological transcription the following nom pl 4th decl nouns:

1. существа́	2. моря́	3. зда́ния

We now turn to the gen pl. According to the chart in (23) there are ten regular gen pl endings, with three being repeated (Ø, *ей*, and *ий*). How many morphemes do we need to represent these ten endings? In 1st decl we easily see the two endings -*ов* and -*ев* as {+ов}, since by the *о ~ е* spelling rule the latter is related to the former as in: *музéев* {музэ́й + ов}. The combination of *й* and unstressed *о* is represented by orthographic *е*: *музéев*. That means first decl has only two gen pl morphemes, {+ов} and {+эй}, the latter seen in, e.g., *учителей*.

The gen pl 2nd decl endings -Ø, -*ь*, and the gen pl 4th decl ending -Ø can all be represented by the same morpheme, namely {+Ø}, as in:

(25) {рэк + Ø}   {нэдэ́л′ + Ø}   {мэст + Ø}
       рек   *недель*   *мест*

Words ending in -*ия* and -*ие* in the nom sg (2nd and 4th decls) have the same gen pl ending, namely, -*ий*. We saw earlier that nouns with these endings in the nom sg all have a stem final *й*. This stem final *й* can be seen in the gen pl. Thus, the gen pl ending for these words must also be zero.

(26) **nom sg**   а́рмия {а́рмий + а}   зда́ние {зда́ний + о}
      gen pl   а́рмий {а́рмий + Ø}   зда́ний {зда́ний + Ø}

We have identified three morphemes for the gen pl: {+ов}, {+эй}, and {+Ø}. There are no others. All orthographic gen pl endings are related to these three. Can we predict when the various endings will occur? Yes.

The gen pl ending {+эй} occurs in three types of nouns. First, it occurs in nouns whose nom sg ends in a soft consonant:

(27)   **1st decl**   **3rd decl**
      nom sg   учи́тель {учи́т′эл′ + Ø}   ло́шадь {ло́шад′ + Ø}
      gen pl   учителéй {учит′эл′ + э́й}   лошадéй {лощад′ + э́й}

Thus if the nom sg ends in a soft consonant, the gen pl ending will be -*ей*.

The gen pl ending {+эй} also occurs in 1st decl nouns whose stem ends in a husher. This is understandable from a historical perspective:

all hushers were once soft consonants. Although ж and ш have become
hard consonants in modern Russian, 1st decl nouns ending in these
sounds as well as other hushers (щ, ч) all continue to take the gen pl
ending {+эй}:

(28) **nom sg**   врач {врач + Ø}   това́рищ {това́рищ + Ø}
     gen pl   враче́й {врач + э́й}   това́рищей {това́рищ + эй}

Notice that this ending is normal for stems that end in a husher **only
among 1st and 3rd decl nouns**. Among 2nd and 4th decl nouns whose
stem ends in a husher, the vowel of the nom sg is usually replaced by
the zero ending: 2nd decl: *ту́ча* ~ *туч*, *ро́ща* ~ *рощ*; 4th decl: *чудо́вище* ~
чудо́вищ.

   Finally, the gen pl ending {+эй} also occurs in two high frequency
4th decl nouns: *мо́ре* ~ *море́й*, *по́ле* ~ *поле́й*, e.g., {мор' + э́й}.

   A rule of thumb is that if the nom sg ends in a soft consonant or
husher, the gen pl ending is {+эй}. First decl nouns whose stems end in
a hard consonant or -*й* take {+ов}, and all others take {+Ø} for the gen
pl. Note that words such as *статья́* – gen pl *стате́й* do not take the
ending {+эй}, as it may appear, instead, they take the zero ending in
the gen pl, as do nearly all nouns that take a vocalic ending in the nom
sg (with the exception of *мо́ре* and *по́ле*, mentioned above):

(29) кни́га   →   gen pl   книг
     неде́ля   →   gen pl   неде́ль
     а́рмия   →   gen pl   а́рмий
     ме́сто   →   gen pl   мест
     статья́   →   gen pl   стате́й

The *e* seen in the gen pl sequence -*ей* in *статей* is a fleeting vowel:

(30) статья́   {стат'/й + а́}   →   стате́й   {стат'/й + Ø}
     семья́   {сэм'/й + а́}   →   семе́й   {сэм'/й + Ø}
     ружьё   {руж/й + о́}   →   ру́жей   {ру́ж/й+ Ø}

The right slash in the transcriptions of (30) represents a fleeting vowel.
We will have much more to say about fleeting vowels in section 6.5.

For now we simply mark the possibility of a fleeting vowel in MT by means of a forward slash /.

The following chart summarizes the rules for the gen pl endings. They assume that the spelling rules account for predictable variations, including the rule *o ~ e*. These rules define the notion "regular" for gen pl. Deviations from these rules, and there are several, are "irregular."

(31) **Genitive Plural Morphemes by Declension Class**

Stem Final Cons	1st Decl	2nd and 4th Decl	3rd Decl
hard or й →	+ ов	+ Ø	
husher →	+ эй	+ Ø	+ эй
soft →	+ эй	+ Ø / + эй[1]	+ эй

[1] The gen pl ending is {+Ø} for 2nd decl nouns and {+эй} for *пóле* and *мóре* (4th decl).

The information in (31) can be simply stated in the following set of rules:

(32) a. The nom sg ends in a vowel → the gen pl is {+Ø} (except *пóле, мóре*)

   b. The nom sg ends in a hard consonant (except hushers) or *й* → the gen pl is {+ов}

   c. The nom sg ends in a soft consonant or husher → the gen pl is {+эй}

Practice

B. Is the gen pl form in the following regular or irregular?

1. стол – столóв
2. падéж – падежéй
3. край – краёв
4. сапóг – сапóг
5. ёж – ежéй
6. богúня – богúнь
7. мелóдия – мелóдий
8. змея́ – змéй
9. свечá – свечéй
10. жилúще – жилúщ
11. нéмец – нéмцев
12. армянúн – армя́н
13. вóлос – волóс
14. солдáт – солдáт

15. ку́хня – ку́хонь
16. страна́ – стран
17. семья́ – семе́й
18. ханжа́ – ханже́й
19. ноздря́ – ноздре́й
20. донесе́ние – донесе́ний

C. Why is the first cell under "3rd Decl" in (31) empty?

D. What is the gen pl of the following words? Write in normal orthography.

1. коро́ва
2. звук
3. ры́нок
4. стиль
5. слу́чай
6. гроза́
7. ли́чность
8. достиже́ние
9. деви́ца
10. иде́я
11. крите́рий
12. душ
13. ситуа́ция
14. слова́рь
15. бога́ч
16. ста́туя
17. ава́рия
18. я́мочка
19. во́йско
20. о́вощ
21. у́лица
22. ту́ча
23. боло́то
24. ружьё
25. вещество́
26. музе́й
27. очеви́дец
28. ло́жа
29. свинья́
30. ключ

E. Write the gen pl forms of the following in morphological transcription.

1. заво́д
2. геро́й
3. мора́ль
4. да́ча
5. душа́
6. кре́сло

4.9. Adjective Endings

Short form adjectives decline for gender only in the sg and these three endings oppose one pl ending:

(33)   sg: бога́т бога́та бога́то   pl: бога́ты

The orthographic endings are identical to those of the 1st (for masc), 2nd (for fem), and 4th decl (for neut) nom sg noun morphemes ({+ Ø} {+ a} {+o}) and to the pl morpheme {+ ы}. Agreement (*согласова́ние*) between short form adjective and noun takes place on the basis of the identity of endings: *Оксáна былá богáта.*

The nom of long form adjectives also shows a correspondence:

(34)	**masc**	**fem**	**neut**	**pl**
hard	ый (óй)	ая	ое	ые
soft	ий	яя	ее	ие

All these endings have one sound in common: [й]. It is the final sound in the masc endings, and occurs in the middle of the fem, neut, and pl endings. The endings in (34) are represented by the following morphemes:

(35)	masc:	{+ый}
	fem:	{+айа}
	neut:	{+ойо}
	pl:	{+ыйэ}

The i-kratkoe seen in the endings in (35) historically was used to form long form adjectives, which differ from the short form in that the former impart a notion of a permanent quality to the sense of the adjective. By adding the -й- to the short form ending and then adding the short form ending again at the end of the sequence, the long form ending was obtained in the nom sg and acc sg fem. This can be seen most clearly in the fem and neut forms, where {+ а й а} = -*ая*, and where {+ о й о} = -*ое*.

The acc sg fem adjective ending also has an й: {+ у й у} = -*ую*. The rest of the long form paradigm copies the pronominal paradigm:

(36)	**masc/neut**	**fem**	**pl**
gen	ого	ой	ых
prp	ом	ой	ых
dat	ом	ой	ым
ins	ым	ой	ыми

Soft variations (nom sg masc -*ий*, fem -*яя*, neut -*ее*, etc.) are due to the spelling conventions discussed in 4.3 (8). In these adjectives the stem ends in a palatalized consonant: {сúн' +ый} = *сúний*.

4.10. Comparative Endings

The simple comparative ending (*-ee*) is represented by the morpheme {+эйэ}: *новее* {нов + эйэ}. A colloquial variant of this suffix is also found, {+эй}: *новей* {нов + эй}. Finally, adjectives ending in a velar (*к, г, х*) take the variant {+э}, with an alternation in the root: *дорогой ~ дороже, яркий ~ ярче*. The variant {+э} is also used for **some** adjectives whose stem ends in the dentals *-т, -д, -с, -ст, -з* or labial *-в* in the long form and show an alternation in the comparative:

(37) | **long form** | | **comparative** |
|---|---|---|
| молодой | ~ | моло́же |
| ни́зкий | ~ | ни́же |
| коро́ткий | ~ | коро́че |
| дешёвый | ~ | дешёвле |

The comparatives in (37) illustrate some of the alternations that occur with dentals, labials, and hushers. Here is the complete set of observed alternations:

(38) | т | ~ | ч | as in | круто́й | кру́че |
|---|---|---|---|---|---|
| д | ~ | ж | " | твёрдый | твёрже |
| з | ~ | ж | " | бли́зкий | бли́же |
| с | ~ | ш | " | высо́кий | вы́ше |
| ст | ~ | щ | " | чи́стый | чи́ще |
| в | ~ | вл | " | дешёвый | дешёвле |

As some examples in (37) and (38) suggest, the adjectival suffix *-к* or *-ок* is often dropped with the abbreviated comparative morpheme {+э}. There are instances when these suffixes are retained, however: *чёткий ~ чётче*. In the following the *-к* is dropped in the comparative, e.g., *у́зкий ~ у́же*.

(39) | га́дкий | га́же | далёкий | да́льше |
|---|---|---|---|
| гла́дкий | гла́же | бли́зкий | бли́же |
| сла́дкий | сла́ще | ни́зкий | ни́же |
| ре́дкий | ре́же | у́зкий | у́же |

жи́дкий	жи́же	то́нкий	то́ньше
глубо́кий	глу́бже	широ́кий	ши́ре

In other -кий adjectives, the -к- alternates with -ч- (*я́рче*). Note most -кий adjectives form no comparative: *ру́сский*, *у́мненький*.

Only a few adjectives form the comparative by means of the -*е* variation. By far the most productive comparative suffix is the full one, even for adjectives ending in labials: *сла́бый ~ слабе́е, глу́пый ~ глупе́е*.

How does morphological transcription handle alternations of the sort *молодо́й ~ моло́же*? The morphological transcriptions:

(40) {молод + о́й}   {моло́ж + э}

suggest there are (at least) **two variants** for the morpheme associated with the sense 'young'. But up to now we have not allowed variations in morphemes. We've explained variations by means of phonological rules. However, there are no phonological rules that account for the alternations in (38), (39), and (40). It appears, therefore, that Russians connect the two variations in (40) as illustrated in (41):

(41)   'young'

{молод-}   {молож-} (comparative)

But surely there is some connection between the -*д*- in *молодо́й* and the -*ж*- in *моло́же*! It is the same *д~ж* alternation we see throughout Russian (*ви́деть ~ ви́жу, сад ~ сажа́ть*). The schema in (41) implies there is no connection at all, other than meaning, between these morphemes. Before discussing further this and similar questions, we must first examine endings in the verbal system, the topic of chapter 5. We will see that verbs often display alternations similar to those seen in the comparatives, which the morphology, as developed to this point, is unable to describe without recourse to further devices.

4.11. Review

The set of endings for nouns makes it possible for nouns to function differently in sentences, without respect to position in the sentence. The four declensional paradigms were inherited from ancient ancestor

languages such as Common Slavic and Indo-European. Syncretism
(identical endings) and principles of morphological transcription per-
mit us to represent the many variations of endings into simple paradigms (e.g., nom sg 2nd decl: *-a, -я, -ия* are all represented by the morpheme {+a}). MT allows us to see the simplicity of the inflectional system where the orthography leads us to believe there are several
endings.

Adjective declension is based on a system of **agreement** with noun
endings, which in some cases, actually have the same vowel repeated
in both adjective ending and noun ending. Alternations in comparatives appear in some adjectives whose stem ends in a velar or labial.

Practice

A. Write the following in morphological transcription.

1. гла́вный
2. дома́шний
3. хоро́шего
4. смета́на
5. княги́нь (gpl of княги́ня)
6. ба́бушек (gpl of ба́бушка)
7. твёрже (comp of твёрдый)
8. умне́е
9. бли́же (comp of бли́зкий)
10. ста́рое

5.1. Introduction

Like the Russian nominal and adjectival inflectional system, many of the complexities of the verbal system can be understood by using morphology as a descriptive device. In this chapter we will first review the facts of verbal inflection as expressed by normal orthography. We will use this to point out a few important generalizations about variant endings which may have previously escaped the student. We will then apply the principles of morphology to the verbal paradigms.

5.2. Present/Future Tense Endings

Unlike nouns, which have four different sets of endings, verbal inflection is limited to two sets of endings (1st conj and 2nd conj) with only four irregular verbs that do not belong completely to either conjugation. Much of the regularity of conjugation can be seen even on the **orthographic** level, which we will review in this section. Conjugation (*спряжёние*) refers to the set of endings a verb takes in the present tense. In this chapter "present tense" refers to conjugation in the present tense and simple (perfective) future. There are three variants of the 1st conj, illustrated as (a), (b), and (c) in (1):

(1) **First Conjugation Endings**

	a.	b.	c.
я	читá + ю	ид + ý	стáн + у
ты	читá + ешь	ид + ёшь	стáн + ешь
он/а/о	читá + ет	ид + ёт	стáн + ет
мы	читá + ем	ид + ём	стáн + ем
вы	читá + ете	ид + ёте	стáн + ете
они	читá + ют	ид + ýт	стáн + ут

While the endings are similar in the three paradigms given above, certain variations are evident. How can we relate the three sets of endings and how do the morphological principles already discussed explain the observed variations?

Looking vertically, the paradigms in (1) show three different sets of endings. However, looking horizontally, we find only two variations. For example, the first sg ending of the verb in (a) differs from those in (b) and (c). In the former the ending is -ю, in the latter the ending is -y. When will it be -ю and when will it be -y? It is clear that stress does not play a role in the choice of endings here, because the ending -ю may occur under stress (даю́) or not and the ending -y may occur with or without stress (ста́ну). For first conj verbs, the ending -y is used when the verbal stem ends in a consonant, -ю when the stem ends in a vowel. The same thing is true for the они́ forms.

The second variation evident in the endings in (1) can be seen in the endings for the ты, он/а/о, мы, and вы forms. In the verbs in (a) and (c) these endings have the vowel -e-, while verbs like those in (b) have a ё. This variation is due to the location of stress. When stress falls on these endings, then the vowel will be -ё-. When stress falls on the stem, then the vowel in the ending is -e-. These differences are all based on information that is part of the verb itself—the location of stress and the type of sound found at the end of the verbal stem.

Practice

A. The following are 1st conj verbs. Conjugate them as in (1):

обозна́ться   вести́   привы́кнуть

So far we have seen that the differences in endings observed in 1st conj verbs, as illustrated in (1) above, are based on features associated with the verb stem or stress.

Consider now several apparent exceptions to the principles regarding the distribution of the endings -ю/y and -юm/ym. There is a set of 1st conj verbs that do not have a vocalic stem in the present tense, that is, their stems do not have a vowel. They all end in -ить in the infinitive: бить, пить, лить, etc. When conjugated, these verbs all have a soft sign: я бью, я пью, я лью. Thus the **stems** of these verbs all end in a (soft) consonant: бь-, пь-, ль-. According to the generalization dis-

cussed above, the ending -*y* should follow a stem ending in a consonant. We can complicate matters by altering the characterization given
above regarding these endings by suggesting that in 1st conj verbs, the
ending -*ю* occurs after vowels **and after soft signs**. This is not too bad,
since, as we will see in chapter 7, the soft sign historically was a vowel.
Inflectional morphology will allow us to eliminate this exception, but
it is valid when dealing just with orthography.

Another apparent exception regarding the endings -*ю/y* and
-*ют/ут* are verbs that have the form -*оротъ* or -*олотъ* in the infinitive.
For example: *боро́тъся ~ я борю́сь*. This is a clear violation to the statement that the ending after consonants is -*y*. Neither of these exceptional classes of verbs (1st conj verbs in -*итъ* or -*оротъ/олотъ* verbs)
will be exceptional when we look in more detail at the morphological
structure of verbs.

Second conj verbs have only two variations in the endings they
use. They occur in the *я* and *они́* forms, as illustrated in (2).

(2) **Second Conjugation Endings**

	a.	b.
я	говор + ю́	спеш + у́
ты	говор + и́шь	спеш + и́шь
он/а/о	говор + и́т	спеш + и́т
мы	говор + и́м	спеш + и́м
вы	говор + и́те	спеш + и́те
они	говор + я́т	спеш + а́т

The spelling rule which states that *ю* and *я* are written as *y* and *a* after
hushers accounts for these orthographic variations.

5.3. Back to First Conjugation: "Regular" Versus "Unusual"

The main structural difference between 1st and 2nd conj verbs is in the
"theme" vowel of the ending. In 1st conj verbs, the theme vowel is either *e* or *ё* depending on stress. Second conj has *u*. Another difference
is in the ending for *они́*. 1st conj has -*ют/-ут* while 2nd conj has -*ят/*
-*ат*. Except for these differences, however, both conjugations are quite
similar. These similarities are shown in (3):

(3) <u>person</u>   <u>structure of ending</u>

я   . vowel

ты   ·   vowel + шь

он/а/о   vowel + т

мы   vowel + м

вы   vowel + те

они́   vowel + т

The consonant part of the endings in (3) are person/number endings.
Note that they are the same for both conjugations. Recall that 1st conj
verbs have the ending -ю/-у in the я form. Orthographic -ю results
from the morphological combination of **soft consonant (including й) +
y**. With this in mind we can break down the я form of 1st conj verbs to
determine its morphological components.

(4) чита́ю   {чит -a -й + y}   1 = root
                  1   2 3   4   2 = verb-forming suffix
                                            3 = present tense marker
                   1,2,3 = stem   4 = ending

We can describe the present tense of all 1st conj verbs as having this
basic structure, although, as we will see, sometimes some of the slots
are empty. In addition, for most forms, there is a "theme" vowel—a
vowel which separates consonants from each other and is part of the
ending. For 1st conj verbs, the theme vowel is {о} (underlined in the
following):

(5) чита́ю   {чит -а́ -й +y}[1]

     чита́ешь   {чит -а́ -й +ош}

     чита́ет   {чит -а́ -й +от}

     чита́ем   {чит -а́ -й +ом}

     чита́ете   {чит -а́ -й +отэ}

     чита́ют   {чит -а́ -й +ут}[2]

---

[1] No theme vowel; y is not a consonant.

[2] No theme vowel; y is not a consonant.

This represents orthographic -ё when stressed and -e when not stressed (*даёшь, читáешь*).

In modern Russian the first sg form (e.g., *читáю*) and third pl form (*читáют*) have no theme vowel. In a distant time past the theme vowel -*o* was present here also but historical sound changes have removed the -*o*- from these forms. The presence of the theme vowel {o} in verbs such as those in (5) defines 1st conj.

There are many 1st conj verbs which appear to be "irregular," but we will see that in fact they are simply a little different—not irregular at all. Some 1st conj verbs are famous for changing the verb-forming suffix in the present tense. Verbs in -*овать* are a good example:

(6) a. {совэ́т -ова +т′}   совéтовать

    b. {совэ́т -у -й +у}   совéтую

    c. {совэ́т -у -й +ош}   совéтуешь

(Note that the present tense marker {+й} is not present in the infinitive or past tense.) The infinitive in (6a) shows the full verb-forming suffix -*ова*- as used in nonpresent forms, and (6b–c) show that the suffix is -*у*- in present tense forms. While this verb is not as simple as, say, *читáть*, it is conjugated in exactly the same way, and, therefore, it is not irregular in conjugation. It simply has an -*у* for its verbal suffix, whereas *читáть* has an -*a*. Russian speakers do have to remember that verbs with the suffix -*ова*- have a peculiarity in conjugation, namely, the suffix -*ова* alternates with -*у* when conjugated. Having made that permutation, the conjugation of these verbs is normal.

Verbs formed by means of the suffix -*ну*- are also conjugated normally. The suffix -*ну*- as seen in the infinitive and past tense has the variant -*н*- when conjugated:

(7) a. {отдóх -нý +т′}   отдохнýть

    b. {отдóх -н +ý}   отдохнý

    c. {отдóх -н′ +óш}   отдохнёшь

In (7a) the full verbal suffix *ну*- is used, while its truncated form *н*- is found in conjugation (7b–c). Note also that the present suffix -*й*- is not used when the stem ends in a consonant. You may be wondering how to account for the soft *н* in *отдохнёшь*. The answer to this question entails a separate area of study within linguistics, and, because of its implications, we will put off its discussion until the next chapter, which is devoted to answering this and similar questions, such as how MT describes comparatives that have an alternation: *молодóй ~ молóже*.

Other unusual (but not irregular!) verb types are illustrated in (8).

(8)	Infinitive in…	Pres Stem	Example	Morphologically
	-ереть	-р	стерéть:	{с=тэрэ́ +т'}
			сотрý	{со=тр +ý}
			сотрёшь	{со=тр' +óш}
			сотрýт	{со=тр +ýт}
	-ыть	-ó	закрýть:	{за=кры́ +т'}
			закрóю	{за=крó -й +у}
			закрóешь	{за=крó -й +ош}
			закрóют	{за=крó -й +ут}
	-давать -ставать	-а́	вставáть:	{вставá +т'}
			встаю́	{вста -й +ý}
			встаёшь	{вста -й +óш}
			встаю́т	{вста -й + ýт}
	monosyllabic -ать, -деть	-н/м	одéть:	{о=дэ́ +т'}
			одéну	{о=дэ́н +у}
			одéнешь	{о=дэ́н' +ош}
			одéнут	{о=дэ́н +ут}
	monosyllabic -ить	-Ø	лить:	{ли́ +т'}
			лью	{л'й +ý}
			льёшь	{л'й +óш}
			льют	{л'й +ýт}

Similarly, verbs in *-чь*, *-сть/зть*, and *-ти* have predictable stems. Once the stem is arrived at, these verbs, as well as those given in (8), are conjugated regularly. For example, the present tense stem of *идти́* and *печь* is {ид-́} and {пэк-́}. Normal endings are added.

(9)	иду́	{ид +ý}		пеку́	{пэк +ý}
	идёшь	{ид' +óш}		печёшь	{пэч +óш}

Note that these verbs also do not take the present tense marker {-й}. The present tense marker only appears when it follows a vowel, as shown in (5–8) above. Two other questions immediately pop up. How does the -∂- in *идёшь* get soft? Similarly, how do we get the -ч- in the verb "to bake:" *ты печёшь*? Again we must beg for patience and ask you to hold these questions until the next chapter. For now we are simply describing what we see in the verb.

Finally, there is a small set of 1st conj verbs whose present tense stems really are odd. These verbs have stems which simply must be memorized; *жить* with pres tense stem {жив-} is a good example. These are "unusual" verbs since they have **unpredictable stems** in the present tense. Still they take the same morphological structure as all other 1st conj verbs and are conjugated normally according to the rules already discussed; thus they are not "irregular," at least as far as their structure or conjugation is concerned.

(10)   жить   {жи +т′}

       живу́   {жив +у́}

       живёшь   {жив′ +о́ш}

The MT in (10) implies that Russians, on some level, know the information in the schema:

(11)   'live'

       {жи- }   {жив- }   {жив′- }

Practice

A. Write in **morphological** transcription:

1. рабо́таю	5. рабо́таешь	9. закажу́
2. зака́жешь	6. собира́ю	10. пьёт
3. начну́	7. сове́тую	11. сове́туешь
4. закро́ю	8. закро́ем	12. забу́дут

B. It was suggested that verbs like *лить* have the stem {л′й-}. Maybe the stem really is {л′-} and the -*й*- in these verbs is actually the present tense marker; *льёшь*, for example, could be {л′ -й +óш}. Why is this not a good idea?

C. Consonant "mutation" in 1st conj verbs usually affects all present (future) tense forms (*сказáть*, but *скажý, скáжешь, скáжет, скáжем, скáжете, скáжут*). What might Russians "know" about the makeup of the root meaning 'to tell'?

5.4. First Conjugation Verb Types

Note that MT solves the problem discussed earlier regarding *ю/ют* occurring after consonants (*бью, борюсь, пошлю*). It shows that morphologically there is only one first sg ending, namely {+y} as seen in all types of 1st conj verbs:

(12)　{чит -á -й + y}　　　читáю
　　　{б′й + y}　　　　　бью
　　　{бор′ + ý -c′}　　　борюсь
　　　{пошл′ + ý}　　　　пошлю

The last two words in (12) require at least some comment. We will want to be able to describe the variation observed in the verbal stems between the infinitive (e.g., *борóться* {борó +т′ -с′a}) and the present tense {бор′-}. The reasons for these alternations can be found in the history of the language (chapter 7), but how can we account for these variations without resorting to history? After all, one may speak Russian fluently without any familiarity at all with the history of Russian. We will attempt to answer this question in chapter 6. For now it is enough to note that these words have at least two root morphemes, e.g.:

(13)　　　'fight'　　　　　　　　　'send'

　　{борó-}*INFIN*　{бор′-}*PRES*　　　{посл-}*INFIN*　{пошл′-}*PRES*

MT allows us to see that endings are regularly added for all verbs. What makes one verb type unusual in comparison with another is **whether or not it takes a particular verbal suffix**. This is the key to understanding the many various shapes verbs can have and to un-locking the simplicity of the verb system. All 1st conj verbs fall into three simple categories described below. Their conjugation capers depend on which category they belong to.

If normal is defined by the number of verbs belonging to a certain class, then the first structure given in (12) above is normal. In that structure each morphological slot is filled. Russian has thousands of verbs with this structure.

The presence and absence of a suffix is binary: + (present), – (absent). In addition, verbs have two stems (past and present). There-fore, there are four possible categories for 1st conj verbs. These are il-lustrated (14). For the purposes of (14), the word "past" stands for both past tense and infinitive.

(14) +/+   suffix is present in both past and present (e.g., *де́ла̲л̲/де́ла̲ю̲*); thousands of verbs

+/–   suffix is present only in the past (e.g., *писа́ть/пишу́, посла́ть/пошлю́*) about ninety verbs

–/+   suffix is present only in the present tense; no verbs

–/–   suffix is absent in both present and past (e.g., *нёс/несу́*); about two dozen

Thus the difference in conjugation between verbs such as *писа́ть* and *де́лать* is due to their morphological structure, not due to differences in conjugation, which is identical for both. *Писа́ть* is a +/– verb, or to be more precise, an *a/Ø* verb, while *де́лать* is a (+/+) or *a/a* verb. *Танцева́ть* is a +/+ verb, and its stem shows an alteration of the verbal suffix: {танц -ова́ +т'} ~ {танц -у́ -й +у}. The verb вы́тереть is a –/–, or to be precise, a *Ø/Ø* verb: {вы́=тэрэ +т'} ~ {вы́=тр +у}. Note that verbs like *вы́тереть* and *нача́ть* do not have a suffix in either past or present tense. Instead, they have an alternating stem. The *a* in the in-finitive of *нача́ть* is part of the root, as is the *н* in the conjugated form: {нача́ + т'} ~ {начн +у́}.

Practice

A. Classify the following verbs as to their morphological structure: +/+, +/–, –/–. For each verb, write out the morphological transcrip-tion for the *я* form.

Example: *понима́ть* +/+ {поним -а -й -у}.

1. страда́ть
2. сочиня́ть
3. старе́ть
4. оде́ть
5. откры́ть
6. пить
7. интригова́ть

8. улыбну́ться
9. стере́ть
10. дава́ть
11. мочь
12. укра́сть
13. вести́
14. снять

B. Conjugate each verb above for я, ты and они́. If you don't know the verb or its structure, look it up.

5.5. Second Conjugation

The structure of 2nd conj verbs is much simpler than that of 1st conj verbs. There is no present tense marker and the suffix {-и} serves as a theme vowel, i.e., the suffix {-и} is part of the ending. The example in (15) is for the verb *говори́ть*, an *и/и* verb.

(15)	говорю́	<	{говор' +у́}
	говори́шь	<	{говор +и́ш}
	говори́т	<	{говор +и́т}
	говори́м	<	{говор +и́м}
	говори́те	<	{говор +и́те}
	говоря́т	<	{говор' +а́т}

The theme vowel -*и* accounts for softness in forms where it occurs. Softness in the я and они́ forms is not predictable, and so must be entered in the morphological transcription. There is a method for explaining softness in these two forms, as well as for softness in forms such as *живёшь*. This method will be the topic of the next chapter. For now, simply note that **stem final consonants of 2nd conj verbs are soft**, whether because of phonology (as in the *ты, он/а, мы, вы* forms) or morphology (as in the я and они́ forms). Of course, *ж* and *ш* remain hard: *реши́ть, решу́, реши́шь*. As in first conj verbs, a spelling rule explains the observed differences in spelling of the 1st sg and 3rd pl endings:

(16) говорю́, решу́ {+у} ~ говоря́т, реша́т {+ат}

Second conj verbs whose stems end in -р, л, н, or a husher do not exhibit an alternation in conjugation. Other 2nd conj verbs, however, do show an alternation, but **in the 1st person sg only**. The alternation is between dental stops and hushers, dental fricatives and hushers, and the addition of an л to labials:

(17) **2nd Conj**	**Dentals**					**Labials**				
final consonant...	д	т	з	с	ст	п	б	ф	в	м
...in 1st sg alternates with	ж	ч	ж	ш	щ	пл′	бл′	фл′	вл′	мл′

Examples: *води́ть ~ вожу́, чи́стить ~ чи́щу, корми́ть ~ кормлю́.*

So, in a real sense many 2nd conj verbs have two present tense stems. For example, for *води́ть* we find {вож-} and {вод-}. The first variant is used in the 1st sg, the second used in all the other forms of the present tense, thus: {вож -у́}, {во́д -иш}. Morphology is about describing how words are put together. In the next chapter we will want to connect the roots {вож-} and {вод-} somehow because they share identical meanings and are much alike, just as we will want to connect the roots *моло́д(о́й)* and *моло́ж(е)*.

Practice

A. Write in morphological transcription:

1. бро́шу
2. бро́сишь
3. смотрю́
4. смо́тришь
5. встре́чу

6. встре́тишь
7. беспоко́ю
8. беспоко́ишь
9. чи́щу
10. чи́стишь

B. Which conjugation, 1st or 2nd, is simpler in terms of ease in predicting the stem, and thus how to conjugate the verb?

C. Some say the 2nd conj verb *чтить* 'to honor' is completely irregular. How is it conjugated? What **should** the 1st sg be? Why isn't it?

D. Write out the following verbs in the *я*, *ты*, and *они* forms:

1. бродить
2. платить
3. ставить
4. благодарить

5. бояться
6. варить
7. обнаружить
8. пилить

5.6. The Infinitive and the Imperative

The infinitive form of most 1st conj and all 2nd conj verbs is arrived at by adding the infinitive suffix -*ть*, -*чь*, -*ти* ({+т'}, {+ч}, {+ти}) to the past tense stem. As we saw earlier, this stem may be exactly like the present tense stem, or it may have a different suffix. In the following examples, the verb-forming suffix is in bold:

(18)	**present tense stem**	**past tense stem**	**infinitive**
	рабо́т -**а**	рабо́т -**а**	{рабо́т -**а** + т'}
	пиш -	пис -**а́**	{пис -**а́** + т'}
	отдо́х -**н**-	отдо́х -**ну́**	{отдо́х -**ну́** + т'}
	твор -**и***	твор - **и́**	{твор -**и́** -т'}
	смотр -**и***	смотр -**э́**	{смотр -**э́** + т'}

*Remember that the suffix -*и*- serves in the present tense also as a theme vowel.

For 1st conj stems that end in a velar (e.g., *могу́*), the infinitive ending is -*чь* ({+ч}) and the velar is absent: *мочь* < {мо +ч}. First conj verbs that stress the ending have -*ти́*: *нести́* < {н'ос +ти} (except for stems ending in a velar: *пеку́, печёшь*). All other verbs take the infinitive ending {-т'}.

There are three orthographic imperative endings: *и*, *ь*, and *й*. Their distribution is predictable orthographically from the present tense stem as illustrated in (19).

(19) **present stem ends in…**   **imperative suffix (orthographic)**

a vowel: й   чита́й

two consonants: и   чи́сти

one consonant and…
    stress on stem: ь   встре́ть
    stress on ending: и   говори́, пиши́

Examples:

(20) a. рабо́тай, сове́туй, закро́й

    b. чи́сти, смотри́, отдохни́, пошли́ (< посла́ть)

    c. брось, заме́ть, забу́дь, вста́нь

    d. говори́, неси́, положи́, закричи́

There appear to be three endings for the imperative, *-й, -и*, and *-ь*. What morpheme(s) represent these endings? Imperatives are formed on the basis of the present tense, so the present tense marker {й} should also be present in the morphological variant. For stems ending in a vowel, we find this to be the case; see the examples in (20a) above. In these verbs the imperative morpheme must be {+Ø}.

(21) {рабо́т -а -й +Ø}   рабо́тай
    {сове́т -у -й +Ø}   сове́туй

For stems ending in two consonants, the imperative morpheme has to be {+и}.

(22) {чи́ст +и}   чи́сти
    {смотр +и́}   смотри́
    {пошл +и́}   пошли́
    {ки́с -н +и}   ки́сни

For stems ending in a single consonant, the situation is a little more complex. If stress falls on the ending, then again the imperative morpheme is {+и}.

(23)   {говор +и́}   говори́

       {отдох -н +и́}   отдохни́

If stress falls on the stem, the the imperative morpheme must be zero.

(24)   {встан' +∅}   встань

          {брос' +∅}   брось

Though the imperative ending for the verbs in (24) is {+∅}, we must still account for the softness evident in these imperatives (see chapter 6). We conclude that there are two imperative morphemes {+и} and {+∅}. The former is used when stress falls on the ending or when the stem ends in two consonants. Everywhere else the morpheme {+∅} is used. In all instances the final stem consonant is soft.

Practice

A. The following verbs have stress on the ending in the imperative. Write out the imperative in normal orthography and in MT.

  1. нести́   5. разверну́ть

  2. смотре́ть   6. снять

  3. положи́ть   7. свисте́ть

  4. посвяти́ть   8. заключи́ть

B. These verbs have stress on the stem in the imperative. Write out the imperative in normal orthography and in MT.

  1. запо́мнить   5. оде́ть

  2. заста́вить   6. доста́ть

  3. подгото́вить   7. посове́товать

  4. изуча́ть   8. плю́нуть

C. Write the imperative for the following verbs—check in a dictionary if you are not sure how they are conjugated.

  1. сотвори́ть   3. испе́чь

  2. улыбну́ться   4. узнава́ть

5. танцева́ть	7. стере́ть
6. бро́сить	8. запо́лнить

5.7. Review

Morphology shows that 2nd conj verbs are much simpler in structure than 1st conj verbs. In addition, we found that some 1st conj verbs have an unpredictable present tense stem, while the present tense stem is always predictable for 2nd conj verbs. Of course the theme vowel which defines 1st and 2nd conjugation differs for each. The four verbs that are neither wholly 1st nor 2nd conj are:

(25) *хоте́ть*: sg is conjugated as a 1st conj verb, pl forms are 2nd conj! (Dialects have *хочу́, хо́чешь, хо́чет, хо́чем, хо́чете, хо́чут* making this a regular 1st conj verb.)

(26) *бежа́ть*: the *я* and *они́* forms are 1st conj, the rest are 2nd!

(27) *есть* and

(28) *дать* have only person/number endings in common with 1st conj, and only somewhat resemble 2nd conj in the pl forms.

The morphological apparatus described so far uncovers much of the simplicity of the nominal and verbal inflectional system. It allows us to look below the surface of the chaos of orthography to see the fairly consistent and straightforward structures of words. We have found that a good understanding of the structure of words can significantly help in the day-to-day business of conjugating verbs and declining nouns and adjectives.

As we have reviewed the inflectional systems of nouns, adjectives, and verbs, we have observed alternations that are not readily described by simple spelling rules or morphological rules. For example, we wondered how the morphology would account for variations in the comparative (*молодо́й ~ моло́же*) and conjugation (*пеку́ ~ печёшь, води́ть ~ вожу́*). We were also perplexed to observe softness in some forms of a verbal stem, while in others a hard consonant prevails, as in *живу́* (hard *-в-*), but *живёшь* (soft *-в-*) or in *вста́ну* but *встань*. We were unable to provide a good reason for the observed alternations in these words. In order to describe these phenomena in a consistent way, we must move forward to another aspect of morphology. This is the subject of the next chapter.

6.1. Introduction

We have observed that an ending might have several variants. We
were able to account for most of these variants by means of rules. For
example, we can account for the alternation in writing of the gen sg
masc endings *-a/-я* by reference to a spelling rule which specifies that
after soft consonants the morpheme {+a} is written as *-я* (see 4.3 (8)). Or
we can account for the difference in spelling in the instr sg masc endings *-ом/-ем* by reference to the *o~e* spelling rule. Some words, however, defied our ability to describe them because their variations are
not readily explainable by either spelling rules or pronunciation rules.
These variations occur in roots or word stems, not in endings. For example, the root morpheme in the word *молодóй* has at least two variants, {молод-} and {молóж-}. The second form is found in the short
comparative adjective, *молóже.* The same thing can be said for the root
morpheme in *писáть,* which also has two variants, {пис-} and {пиш-},
as seen in *писáть ~ пишý.* Russian has no spelling or pronunciation
rule that states that *-д-* alternates with *-ж-* before *-е-,* or that somehow
-с- and *-ш-* alternate before *-у-.*

On the other hand, the alternations in these morphemes are not
random. They occur in words that have similar or identical meanings
and we find the same alternations throughout the language. We note
that these alternations seem to occur when one morpheme stands next
to another **specific morpheme**, not just some sound. For example,
when next to **the comparative suffix** {+э}, some morphemes exhibit an
alternation of {д} and {ж}, but only when standing next to this particular **suffix**.

And, sorry to say, some alternations cannot be accounted for even
by means of this type of explanation. A good example of this is the alternation in *писáть ~ пишý.* One might be tempted to suggest that the
final consonant of the stem is *-ш-* when it stands next to the first per-

son singular verbal ending {+у}. But counter examples show that this is just not the case: несу́. In addition, the same alternation can be seen in combination with other morphemes: пи́шешь, пи́шет, etc. So, it can't just be the ending {+у} that's responsible for this alternation.

How do Russians know when to use {пис-} and when to use {пиш-}? Clearly {пис-} and {пиш-} are related because they have the same meaning and because they alternate in the same verb. It appears that there is just no way synchronically to say when this alternation will occur because there is no pattern to capture.

In this chapter we will try to make sense of alternations that occur with specific morphemes and alternations that seem to have no basis for description at all. This will involve adding a feature to MT making it much more powerful. We will then use this new tool to describe how Russian words are formed using a variety of suffixes.

6.2. Morphemes Versus Phonemes

So far we have been mainly concerned with alternations of two types: phonological alternations such as [к] ~ [г], as seen in снег [сн'эк] and снега [сн'э́гъ] and alternations in grammatical endings as in the inst sg masc endings -ом ~ -ем, both represented by the morpheme {+ом}. In this chapter we will discuss a third type of alternation, one that deals with changes within a morpheme that cannot be accounted for by phonological processes or spelling rules. Specifically we would like to be able to describe the alternations seen, for example, in the final consonant in the morpheme {жив-}, which is pronounced soft when followed by the verbal theme vowel morpheme {o} as in живёшь {жив' +о́ш}. We also want to be able to describe, using the same mechanisms, if possible, variations such as those seen in писа́ть, пи́шешь, молодо́й, моло́же, вста́ну, встань. To do this, we must consider two important units of speech, the **phoneme** and the **morpheme**.

A phoneme (фоне́ма) is a **single** sound that is responsible for a change in meaning. For example, the final consonants in the following morphemes are phonemes in English, since they alter the meaning of each pair: hat – had, has – hath, ham – Hal, hash – hatch. Examples in Russian are the final consonants in: бел, без, бед. In Russian, palatalization (softness) is phonemic—it can be crucial in differentiating meaning: мат – мать, у́гол – у́голь, ломо́т 'aches' gen. pl – ломо́ть 'large slice of bread'. Morphemes are composed of phonemes. While phonemes can change meaning, they themselves do not have meaning.

A morpheme (*морфéма*) is a sequence of phonemes that bears grammatical or lexical meaning. For example, the sequence of sounds {стол-} is a morpheme in Russian, as is {+ы}, which expresses the sense "nom pl." The sounds /с/, /т/, /о/, and /л/ are phonemes but are not morphemes since they bear no meaning on their own.

Recall that **phonological** alternations are automatic—they occur whenever they can, as with akanje, for example. **Morphophonemic** alternations may be automatic, or they may appear to be completely without basis. For the most part morphophonemic alternations occur in the modern language because at some time in the past a phonological rule caused a change in one form of a word but not in another form of the same word. The rule then disappeared from the language, but the change continued on as a fossilized remnant in words. An example in English is the word pair *night* ~ *nocturnal*. Both words go back to the Indo-European root *nōkt- 'night.' A series of phononological changes occurred in Germanic and Old English that shifted Indo-European *nōkt- to Old English *nīht*, and ultimately to the modern English pronunciation where no consonant sound precedes the -*t*. These sound changes are no longer active in modern English, but we still have a trace of the earlier shift of *k to *h in the spelling of modern English *ni_ght_* and can even verify the earlier existence of -*k*- in this word in the borrowing (from Latin) *no_ct_urnal* and in related languages as in German *Na_cht_* 'night'. Russian abounds in such alternations.

Consider the underlined roots in (1).

(1)   a.   пере_смотр_éть   b.   пере_смáтр_ивать

The verbs in (1) provide a good example of a sound change that occurred in the language historically but which is no longer active. However, traces of the sound change can still be found. The root in (1a) is {смотр-}, and in (1b) the root is {сматр-}. These two roots are related: they share the same meaning and are similarly composed. Historically, the addition of the suffix -*ива*- (or -*ыва*-) caused preceding -*о*- to shift to -*а*-. Later this sound change no longer operated in the language (see, for example, *основáть* ~ *оснóвывать*). In the modern language the variation illustrated in (1b) occurs in verbs not on the basis of phonology, but in connection with **another morpheme**, namely {-ыва-}.

When the verbal suffix {-ыва} is added to a root with the vowel {о}, then the {о} usually alternates with {а} as in:

(2) обрабо́тать   обраба́тывать   'work up'
    спроси́ть   спра́шивать   'ask'
    закопа́ть   зака́пывать   'begin to dig, bury'
    уговори́ть   угова́ривать   'persuade'
    устро́ить   устра́ивать   'arrange'
    доко́нчить   дока́нчивать   'finish'

Morphophonemics (*морфоноло́гия*) is the study of the alternations in morphemes (sequences of sounds that have **meaning**) which are not due to contemporary phonological pressures. Spelling rules express relationships between written forms (*с А́нн<u>о</u>й* ~ *с Ната́шей*). Phonological rules express relationships between sounds (*окно́* ~ *о́кна* [ʌкно́] ~ [о́кнъ]). Morphophonemic rules express relationships between morphemes. Thus, we can write a rule to express the alternation exhibited in (2), which is actually the result of an ancient phonological shift, whereby root [o] was lengthened to [ō] when adjacent to this suffix. Subsequently the sound [ō] shifted to [a]. Since contemporary Russian does not have long vowels our synchronic explanation of this alternation cannot make reference to [ō]. Instead we say that a specific **sound alternation** (*o~a* in verb roots) occurs when next to the morpheme {ыва}; that is, there is a "morpho"—"phonemic" alternation, which we express:

(3)   MR (Morphophonemic rule) "ыва"   root{o}:{a} __ {+ыва}$_{d.i.}$

Since we will discuss several morphophonemic rules in this chapter, it will be worthwhile to review how they are written. As shown in (3), we provide a title in English for the rule, here MR "ыва," followed by the rule itself. Material to the left of the colon represents one variant of the alternation. Material to the right indicates the other variant of the alternation. Following this is the morpheme that is "responsible" for the alternation. The rule in (3) states that any root {o} will be realized morphologically as {a} if the d(erived) i(mperfective) suffix {-ыва-} is present. This is not a phonological rule since we cannot base the al-

ternation on any physiological trait of the pronunciation of the suffix
or on regular phonetic processes such as assimilation.

To illustrate how the rule in (3) works, consider the verb *устро́ить*
'to arrange,' d.i. *устра́ивать*. These two words share the same general
meaning. This relationship is reflected in the following schema:

(4)   'arrange'
       _____
   {устро́й-}   {устра́й-}

When Russians want to express the sense 'arrange' they choose one of
the morpheme variants (allomorphs) that is connected with this
meaning (or some other morpheme that has a similar meaning). However, as indicated above, the alternation we see in the root variants in
(4) is not just random. There is a way to connect these two forms beyond just that of the common meaning. There is a real tendency in the
morpheme structure of Russian verbs here, one that we do not want to
miss. The tendency is expressed in the morphophonemic rule given in
(3). Therefore we connect these two variations by a broken line and
mark what morphophonemic rule is responsible for their association:

(5)   'arrange'
        _____
   {устро́й -и +ть}   {устра́й -ыва +ть}
        | |
        L _ _ _ _ _ _ _ _ _ _|
              MR "ыва"

The rule in (3) "works" by formally relating two allomorphs, variants
of the same morpheme. In this way, the allomorphic variants are seen
to be related by rule, and not just related by meaning.

Note that morphophonemic rules differ significantly from phonological rules. For example, here is the softening rule (see section 2.4):

(6) Softening Rule: C'v̈   (where C=paired consonants and
                               v̈=front vowel)

Phonological rules simply state a given fact that corresponds to a
physiologically based speech reality. According to (6), soft consonants
are found before front vowels. The morphophonemic rule in (3), how-

ever, connects two root variants by reference to the morpheme {ыва}. Note that a schema illustrating the softening rule does not make reference to meaning, since phonological alternations occur without reference to meaning at all. An example illustrating (6) could be:

(7)

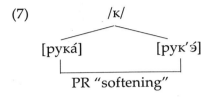

The rule in (6) connects the phonetic alternations ([к] and [к']) found in the two forms. The schema represents this relationship by a solid line, iconic of the inviolable nature of the rule, while the line connecting the morphemes in (5) is broken, suggesting its more restricted nature. It is interesting to note that it is phonological rules (represented by a solid line in our schemas) that are carried over into second language speaking, resulting in accents. Morphophonemic rules, however, are largely language-specific, and do not carry over into a second language. We therefore represent these more tenuous relationships with broken and dotted lines.

6.3. {*o}

It was suggested in chapter 5 that 1st conj verbs have the theme vowel {o}: *читáешь* {чит -á -й -ош}. One of the reasons for this suggestion is that when this vowel is under stress, it is pronounced as an [o]: *живёшь*.

Now consider the stem of the word *идти́*. It presents a set of alternating stem morphemes:

(8) a. идý   {ид +ý}   stem morpheme is {ид-}
                                   (with a hard ∂)

    b. идёшь   {ид' +óш}   stem morpheme is {ид'-}
                                   (with a soft ∂)

These data show us that there are two variations for the root meaning 'to go,' one with a soft ∂ and one with a hard ∂. But, clearly, there is only one word here, *идти́*, with one meaning, only two stem variations. To say otherwise would be to say that the difference between {ид-} and {ид'-} is like the difference between *стол* and *небо*. But if the two stems are variations then we must ask, variations of WHAT? Is one basic and the other derived from it? Historically, yes, one is basic and one is derived from it, as we will see in the next chapter. However, in the modern language Russian speakers go around saying *иду́*, *идёшь* without any knowledge at all about the history of Russian. What **do** they know, if it's not history? They know what they say and what they hear others say. In other words, they simply know there are two root variants for the meaning 'to go,' namely {ид-} and {ид'}. They are connected by meaning and by grammar. We represent this by means of a schema:

(9)   'go'

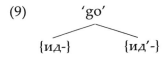

The schema in (9) states that these two roots are related by meaning. We also want to show that they are variants of each other:

(10) MR rule "1CONJ"   к,г,C... : ч,ж,C' __{*o} (where C=paired consonant and {*o} is the 1st Conj theme vowel)

The rule in (10) states that when followed by the 1st conj theme vowel {*o}, к alternates with ч, г with ж, paired consonants with soft variants, and other changes (the three dots indicate there are more sounds involved in this rule; we're just not bothering to list them all at this point). The asterisk means that the alternations we have described are predictable. They always occur in the presence of this morpheme. There is no phonological or spelling rule to account for this sound alternation (consonants do not normally mutate or become soft before the sound [o]). These alternations take place in 1st conj verbs preceding the theme vowel {o}. We can now formally connect the two morpheme variants in (9) by means of this rule:

(11)   'go'

{ид-}   {ид'-}

MR "1CONJ"

The structure in (11) expresses what we think Russians know about
this root. We use a shorthand version of this structure in morphological transcription:

(12)   {ид +ý}
       {ид' +*óш}
       {ид' +*óт}
       etc.

In (12), the asterisk expresses the fact the theme vowel {*o} cooccurs
with soft consonants and hushers (MR "1CONJ") in 1st conj and this
accounts for the softness of the д in conjugation.

Practice

A. Account for the variation in the root of живý ~ живёшь (hard, soft
в).

A similar method can be used to describe the alternations in the
root morphemes of 2nd conj verbs, as in говорю́ ~ говори́шь, which earlier we wrote in MT as {говор' +ý}, {говор +и́ш}. A morphophonemic
rule specifies the 2nd conj ending {+*y} is special: consonants preceding it are soft. We explain similarly "mutations" in 2nd conjugation:
хожý ~ хо́дишь, люблю́ ~ лю́бишь.

(13)   MR "2CONJ"   {т,д,с,р,л,б...} : ч,ж,ш,р',л',бл' ... __{+*y}$_{2nd\ conj}$

The rule in (13) asserts that when morphemes ending in the sounds т,
д, etc. come up against the 2nd conj ending {*y}, they are mapped as
hushers or as soft (for р and л):

(14)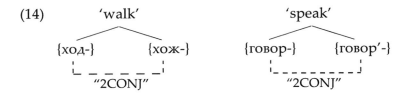

or in our short-hand version: {хож +*ý}, {говор' +*ý}.

Practice

B. Write a morphophonemic rule that would account for softness in 3rd plural forms of 2nd conj verbs: *хо́дят, лю́бят, чи́стят.* (Refer to MR "2CONJ" if you need help.) Don't forget to give your rule an appropriate name. Then write these three words in MT.

C. Write a morphophonemic rule that would relate variations observed in the comparative with the suffix {-э}.

молодо́й ~ моло́же	то́лстый ~ то́лще
ни́зкий ~ ни́же	коро́ткий ~ коро́че
стро́гий ~ стро́же	бли́зкий ~ бли́же

We conclude this section with a discussion of suppletion (*супплетиви́зм*). Suppletion occurs when two words are connected closely by meaning but not connected by phonological or morphological rules. For example in English we have the suppletive pairs:

(15)   person ~ people   go ~ went   I ~ me

Examples of suppletions in Russian are:

(16)   челове́к ~ лю́ди   иду́ ~ шёл   я ~ меня́

These words can only be related by meaning:

(17)   'person'

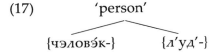

Now consider the variations seen in the following verbs:

писа́ть	пишу́, пи́шешь	{пис-} ~ {пиш-}
сказа́ть	скажу́, ска́жешь	{сказ-} ~ {скаж-}
пря́тать	пря́чу, пря́чешь	{пр'ат-} ~ {пр'ач-}

These forms are really odd. Normally we would expect simple 1st conjugation as in *броса́ть броса́ю, броса́ешъ*. Besides their alternations, these verbs have something else in common, namely, they all have the verbal suffix {+a} in the infinitive but it is missing in the present tense (all are *a/Ø* verbs). The kind of morphophonemic rule we have been using to account for alternations in morphemes is not sufficient to cover these cases. For example, a morphophonemic rule relating these variations by referring to endings {+*y}, {-*oш}, etc., would be incorrect for two reasons. First, there are plenty of counter examples in the *я* forms: *несу́, везу́, мету́*. Second, another morphophonemic rule (MR "1CONJ") contradicts the expected alternations: *несёшъ, везёшъ, метёшъ*. The alternation in the morpheme cannot be explained by the presence of another morpheme. However, if we are allowed to include "other" information in our morphophonemic rules, like reference to verb type, such as *a/Ø verb*, then we can account for these alternations with a **suppletion rule** (SR):

(18)   SR "1 Conj Odd"   root {с, з, т} : {ш, ж, ч} __ {+}*PRES*
                                 (in a/Ø verbs)

The rule in (18) states that *a/Ø* verbs ending in *с, з,* or *m* alternate with *ш, ж, ч*, respectively, in the present tense. Notice that this rule differs significantly from the kind we have been using to account for morphophonemic alternations. In those earlier ones we simply stated the alternation and the morpheme that the alternation was connected with, for example: *∂:ж__+*y* as in {хож +*ý}. The rule in (18), however, makes use of a different kind of information. It specifies the **kind of verb** that exhibits this behavior. (We refer to this as **paradigmatic** information.) The alternation {пис-} ~ {пиш-} is suppletion because it cannot be accounted for by any other kind of rule: spelling, pronunciation, or even morphophonemic. We need paradigmatic information about these verbs in order to see the pattern that they belong to. We will call morphophonemic alternations of this sort **patterned supple-**

tion and agree that the observed alternations are of a different kind than those discussed earlier. Below we illustrate all types of rules:

(19) <u>spelling</u>
         unstressed $o : e$ ж,ш,щ,ц,C' __
                                automatic — no other info needed

      <u>pronunciation</u>
         u : [ы] ж,ш,ц__   **automatic — no other info needed**

      <u>MR rule "1CONJ"</u>
         к,г,C… : ч,ж,C' __{o}   (where {o} is a theme vowel)
                   ↑ **this extra morphological info needed**

      <u>SR rule "1 CONJ ODD"</u>
         root {с, з, т} : {ш, ж, ч} __ {+}$_{PRES}$ (in a/Ø verbs)
                                          ↑ **this paradigm**
                                        info is required

We represent patterned suppletion relationships in schemas by means of a dotted line:

(20)   'write'
             ⌒
   {пис-}   {пиш-}
      ⋮......................⋮
     SR "1Conj Odd"

Note that we are unable to use an asterisk to indicate the relationship expressed in "1Conj Odd" since this really is a pattern based on a lot of variations of a single word (a paradigm), rather than with a single morpheme. Therefore, we write {пис -á +т'} and {пиш +ý}. The stems are different because they are suppletive.

     Finally, recall that the kind of line connecting related alternations in schemas is iconic of the kind of rule involved. A solid line connects alternations in pronunciation and spelling. These are automatic and, since no other information is needed, represent direct, inviolable interactions. In schemas representing morphophonemic relationships, we use a broken line: the interaction is automatic, but information regarding morphemes is required. In schemas representing patterned suppletion we use dotted lines: the connection between the alternations is weakly established in that it requires paradigmatic information. Finally, schemas representing fully suppletive forms (*челове́к~ лю́ди*) have no morphological connection at all—nothing connects them except meaning.

Practice

D. Characterize the following alternations as (m)orphological, (ps) patterned suppletion, or (fs) full suppletion.

1. встре́тить ~ встре́чу	{т}~{ч}
2. купи́ть ~ ку́пят	{п}~{п′}
3. жа́ркий ~ жа́рче	{к}~{ч}
4. маха́ть ~ ма́шешь	{х}~{ш}
5. плеска́ть ~ плещу́	{ск}~{щ}
6. пеку́ ~ печёшь	{к}~{ч}
7. год ~ лет	{год-}~{лэт-}
8. несу́ ~ несёшь	{с}~{с′}
9. люби́ть ~ люблю́	{б}~{бл′}
10. нау́ка ~ нау́чный	{к}~{ч}

6.4. Alternations in Derivation

English often names a new item by means of putting two words together (*haircut, headphones, snowflake*). While Russian also has compound words, it has built much of its new vocabulary upon the foundation of words that already existed in the language by means of adding a suffix (*стри́жка, нау́шники, снежи́нка*). The result is that in Russian, roots show "mutations" or alternations from one word to another (*стри́чься, у́хо, снег*). Are these alternations simply random or can we connect alternating roots by means of morphology?

Most Russian words have the following structure (elements in parentheses may or may not be present in any given word):

(21)   (prefix)   = root   - (suffix)   + ending
        (*приста́вка*)=*ко́рень* - (*су́ффикс*) + *оконча́ние*

Words have at least a root and an ending. Prefixes and suffixes may or may not be present. Examples:

(22) свобóд +a   (root+ending)
      свобóд -н +ый   (root-suffix+ending)
      о=свобод -и́ +ть   (prefix=root-suffix+ending)
      о=свобожд -э́ний + о   (prefix=root-suffix+ending)

In (22) the word *свобóда* is composed of a noun root plus an ending. It is not a derived noun, since it neither contains a suffix nor is the grammatical category of the whole word different from that of the root. The other three words in (22) are derived. Though today they are independently occurring words, they owe their existence to someone in the past adding a suffix to the root. For example, *свобóдный* is an adjective derived by means of the adjective-forming suffix {-н-}; *освободи́ть* is also derived and bears the verb-forming suffix {-и-} as well as a verbal prefix; *освобождéние* is a noun derived from the verb. Note its meaning is somewhat different from that of the original (nonderived) noun. Words may be nonderived or derived from nouns (denominal), from adjectives (deadjectival), or from verbs (deverbal). Thus, *морячóк* 'little sailor' is derived from *моря́к* 'sailor,' which is derived from *мóре* 'sea' (nonderived).

A nonderived word (*непроизвóдное слóво*) is a verb, noun, or adjective without a suffix. Examples of nonderived words are given in (23):

(23)
Root	Occurs in	Gloss
стол-	стол	'table'
книг-	кни́га	'book'
мор'-	мóре	'sea'
бэр-	беру́	'I take'
п'ок-	пеку́	'I bake'
чт-	чту	'I honor'
стар-	стар	'old'
груб-	груб	'rude'

Since suffixes are not involved in the formation of these words, we do not find any morphophonemic alternations.

By adding a suffix, other nouns, verbs, and adjectives have been formed. Examples:

(24)	Root	Suffix	Occur in	Gloss
	стол-	-ик	сто́лик	'little table'
	кни́г-	-к	кни́жка	'brochure'
	мо́р'-	-ак	моря́к	'sailor'
	бэр-	-а	собира́ть	'collect'
	п'ок-	-а	допека́ть	'bake until done'
	чт-	-и	чтить	'to honor'
	ста́р-	-эн'к	ста́ренький	'somewhat old'
	груб-	-оват	грубова́тый	'a bit rude'

More than one suffix may be added, e.g., the diminutive *кни́жечка*. As can be seen in this example, derivation may be accompanied by an alternation in a root or stem. In the remainder of this chapter we will study variations in morphemes that accompany suffixation.

Practice

A. Give the roots for the following words. Write N for nonderived words and D if the word is derived.

1. а́вгуст
2. ста́ну
3. и́щешь
4. ры́ба
5. мо́стик

6. земля́
7. дворе́ц
8. письмо́
9. рыба́к
10. ме́сто

B. For each of the following write (a) the root, (b) any suffix in the word, and (c) another word that has the same root.

1. моря́к
2. сове́товать
3. слова́цкий
4. де́тство

5. столи́чный
6. мучени́к
7. перестро́йка
8. учи́тельница

9. семе́йный
10. тишина́
11. откры́ть
12. нау́ка

C. What general alternation is observable in all the roots of the following derivationally related pairs?

1. стол ~ сто́лик
2. ме́сто ~ месте́чко
3. ход ~ ходи́ть
4. брат ~ бра́тец
5. ры́ба ~ рыбёшка
6. род ~ ро́дина

6.5. Verb Formation

In this section we will examine what alternations occur with verb suffixes. The following patterns are encountered:

(25) a. hard consonants ~ soft variants

b. soft consonants ~ hard variants

c. velars ~ hushers

d. no alternations

For the purposes of verbal derivation, and later noun derivation, we will be able to group all alternations into just two categories, those that are predictable based on the presence of another morpheme (morphophonemic alternations) and those that are not predictable (suppletive alternations).

Verb suffixes have grammatical meaning: they mark words as verbs. For example, the infinitive *чита́ть*, and present tense *чита́ю* have the morphological structure:

(26) {чит -á +т′}   {чит -á -й +у}

The verbal suffix in both is {-a}. Another way of representing this suffix is *a/a*, where the suffix used for past tense and infinitive is given before the slash, the present (and simple future) tense suffix is given after the slash (see section 5.4).

In this section we will examine the following suffixes:

(27) **1st Conjugation**

а/а	as in	чита́ть, отдыха́ть
ова/у		сове́товать, торгова́ть
а/Ø		писа́ть, сказа́ть
э/э		боле́ть, име́ть
ну/н		отдохну́ть, взви́згнуть
Ø/ну/н		поги́бнуть, пога́снуть
ыва/ыва		пересма́тривать, перечи́тывать

(28) **2nd Conjugation**

и/и	as in	гото́вить, испра́вить
а/и		слы́шать, стоя́ть

6.5.1. Verbs in *a/a*

All types of consonants occur with this suffix, including velars and hushers.

(29) a. hard consonants: обе́дать, де́лать, броса́ть

  b. soft consonants: гуля́ть, теря́ть, смея́ться

  c. velars: пуга́ть, возника́ть, пиха́ть

  d. hushers: продолжа́ть, облегча́ть, слу́шать

As indicated in (29c) and (29d) this suffix may follow a velar **or** a husher. Why is this interesting? Because it seems the root morphemes in *продолжа́ть, облегча́ть,* and *слу́шать* are related to the roots that end in a velar: *до́лго, лёгкий, слух*. But if we were to relate these roots by some MR, then the same rule would anticipate verb forms such as **пужать, *возничать,* and **пишать*—all non-occurring forms—instead of what we do get as in (29c). This leads us to the unavoidable conclusion that the root morphemes in pairs such as *до́лго~продолжа́ть, лёгкий~облегча́ть,* and *слух~слу́шать*, while certainly close in meaning and definitely related historically, must be treated as **morphologically** unrelated roots in modern Russian. Similarly, Modern English *might* and *may* must be treated as separate words in the description of English morphology, though they both derive from a common historical source and mean almost the same thing.

Practice

A. How would you write *продолжа́ть* and *слу́шать* in MT?

Similarly, at first glance it does seem that there must be a regular alternation in the following pairs:

(30) **perf**   **derived imperfective**

заме́тить	заме<u>ча́</u>ть
разря<u>ди́</u>ть	разря<u>жа́</u>ть
при<u>гласи́</u>ть	при<u>глаша́</u>ть
уни́<u>зи</u>ть	уни<u>жа́</u>ть

However, these alternations are not completely predictable. We can't simply suggest that root morphemes ending in a dental alternate with hushers in *a/a* verbs (counterexamples abound: *лета́ть, обе́дать, броса́ть, исчеза́ть*.) For now the best we can do is call this a form of suppletion. The verbs *заме́тить* and *замеча́ть* must be considered as different words in the modern language, {за=мэ́т-и+т'}, {за=меч-а́+т'}.

Practice

B. Do the alternations in (30) reflect patterned suppletion? (cf. 6.3 (20))

C. Even though the alternations in (30) are not completely predictable, there is a regularity or pattern to it. What is it?

D. Write the derived imperfective forms of the following perfectives and mark stress:

1. зарази́ть	6. сооруди́ть	11. ослепи́ть
2. отве́тить	7. разреши́ть	12. ознако́мить
3. пригласи́ть	8. упрости́ть	13. укра́сить
4. вста́вить	9. округли́ть	14. победи́ть
5. запрети́ть	10. согласи́ть	15. награди́ть

6.5.2. Verbs in *ова/у*

All alternations connected with this suffix are explained by the spelling rule *о~е*. There are usually no alternations: *совéтовать, комáндовать, образовáть, атаковáть, торговáть, страховáть*. But when next to a soft paired consonant, a palatal, or *ц*, then the suffix-initial *о* shifts to *е* according to the spelling rule: *трелевáть* (cf. *трель*), *горевáть* (cf. *гóре* < {гóр′ +о}) *ночевáть, танцевáть, свежевáть, бушевáть*.

The verbs in (31) illustrate the fact that fleeting vowels with this suffix (as with any suffix beginning with a vowel) are fugitive:

(31)   танцевáть   {танц -ова +т′}

         кольцевáть   {кол′ц -ова +т′}

Some verbs that end in *-евать* do not take the suffix {-у} in the present tense; instead, they are *a/a* verbs: *надевáть, навевáть* 'to blow', *зевáть*. These verbs do not have the suffix *-ова*. The sequence *-ев* is part of the root morpheme, e.g., {зэв -а + т′}.

Practice

A. Write out in morphophonemic transcription and in normal orthography the infinitive with the following root morphemes (they are all normal *ова/у* verbs):

1. {слэ́д-} cf. след
2. {п′йáнств-} cf. пьянство
3. {тáн/ц} cf. тáнец
4. {врач-} cf. врач
5. {тоск-} cf. тоскá

6. {бэ́дств-} cf. бéдствие
7. {брак-} cf. брак
8. {свин/′ц-} cf. свинéц
9. {бэсэ́д-} cf. бесéда
10. {имэн-} cf. и́мя, именá

6.5.3. Verbs in -a/Ø

(32) писа́ть   ~   пишу́   'write'
      слать   ~   шлю   'send'
      ре́зать   ~   ре́жу   'cut'
      глода́ть   ~   гложу́   'gnaw'
      лепета́ть   ~   лепечу́   'babble'

We account for the alternations seen in these verbs as patterned suppletion (see section 6.3).

The verb *стлать* 'set, spread' appears to have a fleeting vowel
which disappears in the past tense and infinitive. We expect this because a vowel follows in these forms. However, the present tense
forms also have a vowel but here the fleeting vowel is present (see
section 6.5.8)!

(33) стлать   {стл -a + т'}   no fleeting vowel when
                                       another vowel follows

      стелю́   {стэл' + у́}   "fleeting" vowel even though
                                       another vowel follows

This root does not have a predictable fleeting vowel. It simply has two
variants of the root in a suppletive relationship (see section 6.5.8).

6.5.4. Verbs in -э/э

Consonants are soft with these morphemes: *сла́бый* → *ослабе́ть*, *зуб* →
обеззу́беть. Though hushers do occur with this suffix, e.g., *свеже́ть*,
they do not represent an alternation; there is no {свэг-} or {свэд-}.

6.5.5. Verbs in -ну/н and -Ø/ну/н

There are two kinds of -нуть verbs. In both kinds the suffix loses the
vowel -у- in the present/future tense: *отдохну́ть, я отдохну́, ты
отдохнёшь*, etc. The suffixes differ in that in one kind the suffix {-ну}
occurs in the past tense:

(34) **-ну/н verbs**

infinitive	past	
клю́нуть	клю́нул	'peck'
верну́ться	верну́лась	'return'
дви́нуть	дви́нуло	'move'
подчеркну́ть	подчеркну́ли	'underline'

In the other kind the suffix {-ну} disappears completely in the past tense (thus -Ø/ну/н means past tense/infinitive/present tense):

(35) **-Ø/ну/н verbs**

infinitive	past	
привы́кнуть	привы́к	'be accustomed'
зати́хнуть	зати́хла	'abate'
со́хнуть	со́хло	'be parched'
подо́хнуть	подо́хли	'die'

The lack of this suffix {-Ø} in the past tense entails no morpho-phonemic alternations. Interestingly enough, consonants are hard before the suffix -ну- (compare ныря́ть {ныр'-} but нырну́ть, грязь {гр'аз'-} but погря́знуть), with the exception of [л'], which remains soft (стрельну́ть). (We will see that л is normally soft in conjunction with other suffixes that begin with -н.)

The adherence of a -нуть verb to the -Ø/ну/н subgroup is predictable on the basis of the following:

(36) a. stress falls on the root morpheme **AND**
     b. the root morpheme ends in a consonant **AND**
     c. the verb is imperfective **OR** the verb is prefixed

For examples, see (35) above. If a -нуть verb has stress on the suffix or the root does not end in a consonant, then it is a -ну/н verb. There are six exceptions to (36): вспы́хнуть, всхли́пнуть, приплю́снуть, проти́снуться, взви́згнуть, all of which should be Ø/ну/н verbs, but which take the suffix in the past. The sixth exception is увя́нуть 'to fade' which has past увя́л, etc. An important caveat to (36) is that prefixed derived verbs of -ну/н verbs are always -ну/н: кли́кнуть (perf) ~ воскли́кнуть (восклиќнул).

Practice

A. Give the past tense masc of the following.

1. сла́бнуть (impf)	6. захлебну́ться
2. просну́ться	7. поги́бнуть
3. привы́кнуть	8. пры́гнуть (perf)
4. замёрзнуть	9. дви́нуть (perf)
5. щёлкнуть (perf)	10. поддёрнуть

The past tense of поддёрнуть is поддёрнул, but it is derived from дёрнуть (perf, hence ну/н).

6.5.6. Verbs in -ыва-/-ива-

This suffix is found in imperfectives related to corresponding prefixed perfectives. It occurs in these two variants, but one variant, -ива-, can be explained by spelling rule: following velars and hushers and when the verb root ends in a soft consonant, the -ива- variant is written (see sections 4.3 (8) and 4.4). Thus, with a handful of rare exceptions, 2nd conj perfective verbs have imperfective partners with the suffix -ива-, since the roots of these verbs are soft, e.g., оцени́ть ~ оце́нивать. The MT for the latter must, therefore, be {оцэ́н' -ыва +т'}. This implies two allophones for the meaning 'evaluate:' {о=цэн-} and {о=цэн'-}$_{IMPERF}$, but they are related by phonological rule.

The suffix {ыва} has two more interesting features. First, stress falls on the syllable preceding it. Second, root vowel -o **after hard consonants** normally alternates with -a in conjunction with this suffix (see section 6.3). Examples:

(37) **prefixed perfective**   **derived imperfective**

пересмотре́ть	пересма́тривать	'revise'
закопа́ть	зака́пывать	'bury'
обрабо́тать	обраба́тывать	'work up'
разлома́ть	разла́мывать	'break down'

Words with the suffix -ова- are not exceptions, since the -о- is not part of a root:

(38) запакова́ть   запако́вывать   'pack'
       реорганизова́ть реорганизо́вывать 'reorganize'
       преобразова́ть   преобразо́вывать   'transform'
       завоева́ть   завоёвывать   'conquer'
       зарисова́ть   зарисо́вывать   'sketch'

And, consider the vowel in the root morphemes of the following:

(39) оскребе́ть   оскрёбывать   'scrape around'
       захлебну́ть   захлёбывать   'swallow down'
       замета́ть   замётывать   'baste'

The root vowel in these words is *o*, but it follows a soft consonant: {оскр'об -а́ + т'} {оскр'о́б -ыва +т'}. The following MR indicates when -*a*- is found in these stems (compare with an earlier and incomplete version in 6.3 (10)):

(40) MR "ыва"   root{o} : {a} C__ {+*ыва}$_{d.i.}$
                      (where C=hard paired consonant)

The rule in (40) states that **root vowel** {...о...} following a hard paired consonant alternates with {...а...} in connection with the suffix -*ыва*, but no other *o*'s do, as illustrated by (38) and (39). Since the suffix -*ыва* is "responsible" for this alternation, we can mark it so in MT: *зака́пывать* {за=ка́п -*ыва +т'}.

Finally, consider this set of alternations:

(41)   загла́дить   загла́живать

        просвети́ть   просве́чивать

        присади́ться   приса́живаться

        угото́вить   угота́вливать

At first glance, it may seem these are like *оцени́ть ~ оце́нивать* {о=цэн -и́ +т'}, {о=цэ́н' -ыва +т'}, whose roots are related by rule. The rule that relates the two forms just given, however, is the softening rule C'ў. We have no rule that could relate *-д-* and *-ж-* before the suffix *-ыва-*, since Russian has plenty of words like *докла́дывать*. In order to predict the alternations visible in (41), we need more information—namely that the imperfective is related to a 2nd conj perfective verb. This is paradigmatic information, which means we are dealing with suppletion—pairs of words related in meaning, but which cannot be shown to be morphological variants of each other.

Practice

A. The following perfectives have derived imperfective partners with {-ыва}. Write out in normal orthography the derived imperfective for each.

1. огороди́ть	9. заворожи́ть
2. опозда́ть	10. допры́гать
3. обусло́вить	11. спроси́ть
4. заторгова́ть	12. описа́ть
5. залечи́ть	13. вы́растить
6. подчеркну́ть	14. опроста́ть
7. договори́ть	15. засвети́ть
8. оспо́рить	16. дорабо́тать

6.5.7. Verbs in *и/и*

This suffix forms 2nd conj verbs. The following alternations occur

(42) a. Consonants are soft with these morphemes:

рубить   {руб -*и́ + т'}
освободить   {о-свобод -*и́ + т'}
числить   {чи́сл -*и+ т'}

(Note: the asterisk in these forms does not refer to softening, which is automatic, but to the alternations seen in (42b).)

(42) b. Velars alternate with hushers:

обслужи́ть   {об=служ -*и́ + т'}   cf. слуга́
смягчи́ть   {с=м'агч -*и́ + т'}   cf. мя́гкий
оглуши́ть   {о=глуш -*и́ + т'}   cf. глухо́й

The verbal suffix {-*и} is marked with an asterisk wherever it occurs, even if the effects of the MR are not felt in any given verb, such as is the case in (42a).

Practice

A. What и/и verbs are related to these words?

1. сла́ва	11. кре́пкий
2. гото́вый	12. царь
3. награ́да	13. ве́ра
4. клей	14. бес
5. мно́го	15. свет
6. ито́г	16. рыба́к
7. гроза́	17. поко́й
8. весёлый	18. грех
9. тёмный	19. сухо́й
10. дво́е	20. му́ка

B. Write the morphophonemic rule that expresses the alternations observed in (42b). Be sure to give your rule a name. For extra credit, draw a schema that relates the meaning and morphology of *обслужи́ть* and *слуга́*.

6.5.8. Verbs in *a/и*

The roots of all but a few verbs taking this suffix end in a husher. Not all verbs ending in a husher are of this type, however, cf. *отвечáть*, an *a/a* verb. Here are several *a/и* verbs that do not end in a husher: *гнать (гоню́, го́нишь), спать (сплю, спишь)*, and *стоя́ть (стою́, стои́шь)*. The paradigm of *гнать* suggests the presence of a fleeting vowel, and certainly this was the case historically. However since the *я* form *гоню́* is exceptional (see the discussion on fleeting vowels in section 6.7) we suggest that for this verb Russian speakers simply have two suppletive roots {гн-} for nonpresent forms and {гон-} for the present tense—same as for *стлать-стелю́*, an *a/Ø* verb.

Nearly all the verbs in this class are intransitive (except *слы́шать* and *держáть*) and denote something to do with noise. Examples follow.

(43) -ЧАТЬ

молчáть	'be quiet'	мчать	'rush, whish'
урчáть	'rumble'	кричáть	'cry'
звучáть	'sound'	ворчáть	'growl'
рычáть	'snarl'	бурчáть	'mumble'
стучáть	'knock'	бренчáть	'jingle'
журчáть	'babble'	мычáть	'moo'

-ШАТЬ

шуршáть	'rustle'	слы́шать	'hear'

-ЩАТЬ

верещáть	'squeal'	трещáть	'crackle'

-ЖАТЬ

дребезжáть	'tinkle'	жужжáть	'buzz'
брюзжáть	'grumble'	визжáть	'squeal, yelp'

Practice

A. Given the following data, write

    (a) the suffixes found in each verb

    (b) the infinitive in MT

    (c) an explanation for observed alternations

For example, the answer to #1 is: (a) *a/Ø*, (b) {плак -а +т'}, (c) SR "1CONJ ODD"

Infinitive	1st sg	2nd sg	Related
1. пла́кать	пла́чу	пла́чешь	пла́кса
2. плати́ть	плачу́	пла́тишь	платёж
3. реша́ть	реша́ю	реша́ешь	реши́ть
4. просвеща́ть	просвеща́ю	просвеща́ешь	просвети́ть
5. облегча́ть	облегча́ю	облегча́ешь	лёгкий
6. треща́ть	трещу́	трещи́шь	треск
7. упако́вывать	упако́вываю	упако́вываешь	упакова́ть
8. осле́пнуть	осле́пну	осле́пнешь	слепо́й
9. разы́скивать	разы́скиваю	разы́скиваешь	иска́ть

B. Give the derived imperfective in *-ыва* (or *-ива*) for the following and be sure to mark stress:

1. насоса́ть	6. выхолости́ть
2. спроси́ть	7. показа́ть
3. доигра́ть	8. наве́сить
4. оправда́ть	9. загада́ть
5. образова́ть	10. устро́ить

6.6. Fleeting Vowels

The time has come for us to face squarely the question of fleeting vowels. We have put off this moment until now because, though there are phonological aspects of the fleeting vowel question, in modern Russian it is essentially a morphophonemic phenomenon.

One of the most striking sound alternations in Russian is its vowel ~ zero alternation. The following word pairs exhibit this alternation.

(44) **nom sg**   **gen sg**

отéц   отцá

рот   рта

мох   мха

лёд   льда

день   дня

сон   сна

The words in the left column in (44) have the vowel *e, o*, or *ë* which disappears in the gen sg forms of the same words. The vowels which alternate with Ø are often referred to as "fleeting" or "unstable" vowels. There are about 19,335 different words in Russian that have a fleeting vowel in at least one form of the word. Words with fleeting vowels occur in all grammatical categories. The gen pl of fem and neut nouns often has a fleeting vowel, as shown in (45) below. As illustrated, fleeting vowels do not have to be stressed when they appear.

(45) **nom sg**   **gen pl**

лóдка   лóдок

окнó   óкон

письмó   пúсем

крéсло   крéсел

тюрьмá   тюрем

Fleeting vowels are also seen in verbal forms and short form adjectives.

(46) звать   зовý   брать   берý

пришлá   пришёл   больнá   бóлен

As indicated above the fleeting vowel is orthographically *o, ë, or e*.

Russians know when a fleeting vowel occurs by comparing variants of a single word:

(47)   'sister'

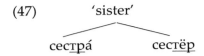

 сестра́   сестёр

This schema asserts that the word that expresses the sense 'sister' has two variants in Russian. We want to know:

(i)   in what words do fleeting vowels occur;

(ii) what forms they show up in;

(iii) when will it be *ё, o,* or *e.*

To answer the questions in (i) and (ii), we observe that fleeting vowels always occur between two consonants and when no other vowel follows. (When another vowel follows, the fleeting vowel disappears.) Unfortunately no good rule exists that allows us to predict completely in what words a fleeting vowel will occur. In modern Russian it is an idiosyncratic feature of many words, though most fleeting vowels are found in suffixes. We offer the following:

(48)   Categories of words with fleeting vowels:

   a.   ten monosyllabic masc nouns:
        лоб, ров, лёд, лён, сон, пёс, рот, мох, лев, день

   b.   short form masc adjectives with the suffix *-к-* (not *-ск-*):
        бли́зкий ~ бли́зок, го́рький ~ го́рек, ре́дкий ~ ре́док

   c.   short form masc adjectives with the suffix *-н-* (not *-н'-*):
        спосо́бный ~ спосо́бен, кра́сный ~ кра́сен, у́мный ~ умён

   d.   a few short form masc adjectives whose stems end in *-р* or *-л*:
        хи́трый ~ хитёр, о́стрый ~ остёр, во́стрый ~ востёр, шу́стрый ~ шустёр, тёплый ~ тёпел, ки́слый ~ ки́сел, све́тлый ~ све́тел

   e.   3 short form end stress adjectives (in *-о́й*):
        дурно́й, хмельно́й, больно́й (ду́рен, хме́лен, бо́лен)

(48) f. thousands of masc nouns with the suffix *-ец* or *-ок*:
          оте́ц ~ отца́, зубо́к ~ зубка́

      g. thousands of 2nd decl and 4th decl nouns with the suffix
          -к-:
          студе́нтка ~ студе́нток, око́шко ~ око́шек

      h. hundreds of disyllabic, nonsuffixed, nouns:
          свёкор ~ свёкра, сестра́ ~ сестёр, сосна́ ~ со́сен

      i. in the stem of a handful of verbs:
          брать ~ беру́, звать ~ зову́, шёл ~ шла

      j. in a few verbal prefixes: *отпере́ть ~ отопру́*

This is really no more than a (not very useful) list of word types. The question of "why" fleeting vowels occur in just these words will be treated in chapter 7.

We transcribe all fleeting vowels with the symbol {/} in morphological transcription, as, for example, in *ска́зка* {ска́з/к +а}, the gen pl *ска́зок* would be {ска́з/к +∅}. This symbol simply represents the fact that sometimes (when no other vowel follows) the word has a fleeting vowel, otherwise there is no vowel present. Since the type of fleeting vowel can be fairly well predicted on phonological grounds, it might be suggested that a rule of the type in (49) relates these alternations.

(49) possible rule "fv"

      a. {/} : {o}   (when no vowel follows and if bounded by *к, г, х*
                       -or-
                       stressed and before a hard consonant)
      b. {/} : {ə}   (elsewhere, as long as no vowel follows)

This rule expresses what the term {/} stands for when it is realized as a vowel. As you can see, the forward slash can stand for either {o} or {ə}, depending on what sounds are around it. We are thus able to describe the word *ска́зка* as containing the morphemes {ска́з/к-} and {+а}, or simply {ска́з/к +а}. The same root morpheme is used in other forms of the word, e.g., *ска́зок* {ска́з/к +∅}. Since no vowel follows the morpheme with the fleeting vowel symbol, the rule "fv" maps out what the {/} stands for in this word. It should be noted that this rule of thumb is most accurate when dealing with fleeting vowels in a suffix or at the end of the stem. It is less useful for fleeting vowels in the root.

Practice

A. Following are some 2nd decl and 4th decl nouns in the nom sg. All take a fleeting vowel in the gen pl. What fleeting vowel should occur in the gen pl of these nouns according to the rule in (49)?

1. подсти́лка	6. дере́вня
2. ка́пля	7. полотно́
3. число́	8. семья́
4. ку́хня	9. ма́сло
5. ку́кла	10. ко́шка

B. Note that the MT of *ко́шек* is {ко́ш/к +Ø}. The proposed rule "fv" suggests that this MT represents {ко́шок +Ø}. Why is the second {о} written -*е*- in the orthographic representation of this word?

The second part of the fv rule expressed in (49a) states that the fleeting vowel will be {o} when it is stressed and before a hard consonant. Here are some examples:

(50) умён {ум/'н +Ø}   fem sg   умна́

сестёр {сест/'р +Ø}   nom sg   сестра́

A major exception to the proposed fv rule occurs when the final member of the consonant cluster is *ц*. Then the fleeting vowel is always *e*, whether under stress or not.

(51) не́мец   не́мца

кольцо́   коле́ц

иностра́нец   иностра́нца

молоде́ц   молодца́

Finally, note that in a handful of words the fleeting vowel is *и*: *оди́н ~ одна́, копьё*, gen pl *ко́пий*.

6.7. Noun and Adjectival Derivation

Now that we understand how fleeting vowels operate, we turn our attention to noun and adjective suffixes. In verbal derivation we saw that some types of morphophonemic alternations are regular and can be described by means of a morphophonemic rule. Root morphemes may have several variants but are structurally related:

(52)   'finish speaking'

{до=говор-}   {до=говар-}

└ — ‾‾MR ″ыва″‾ — ┘

In this section we will review some of the morphophonemic alternations that occur in nominal and adjectival derivation. They can be described using the same kinds of devices that we have become used to: morphophonemic rules that relate alternating forms and schemas that show how the rules work. With nouns and adjectives we find the following types of variations:

(53) a. hard consonants ~ soft variants

     b. velars ~ hushers

     c. soft consonants ~ hard variants

     d. no alternation

Dental consonants do not show alternations in nouns and adjectives, unlike in verbs where we found alternations involving dentals rampant. Here we will see a few dentals that alternate with hushers, but these are suppletions. We will study the following suffixes:

(54) NOUN SUFFIXES

    1. -ец

    2. -ик, -ник, -чик, -щик

    3. -анин

    4. -к

    5. -н(ие)

    6. -ок, -ёк, -онок

    7. -ость

    8. -ств(о)

    9. -тель

(54) ADJECTIVE SUFFIXES

    1. -н(ый)   2. -ск(ий)

6.7.1. Nouns in -ец {-/ц}

This suffix forms agentive nouns, diminutives and nouns showing residency or nationality (e.g., *гавáец* 'Hawaiian'). As discussed above, the fleeting vowel in this suffix is always realized as {э}. When the fleeting vowel is present, preceding consonants are soft as expected according to the phonological rule "softening." Examples:

(55) саýдовец   'Saudi'   {саýдов -/ц +∅}

      чикáгец   'Chicagoan'   {чикáг -/ц +∅}

      ирáкец   'Iraqi'   {ирáк -/ц +∅}

The last two examples in (55) indicate that an alternation between velars and hushers which used to accompany this suffix is no longer an option in modern Russian. Consider, for example, pairs such as *лжец* 'liar' ~ *лгать* 'to lie' and *норвéжец* ({норвэ́ж-/ц+∅}) ~ *Норвéгия*. Because these alternations are not accountable by rule, Russian speakers simply have two (suppletive) roots for each meaning, e.g., {лг-}$_{VERB}$ and {лж-}$_{NOUN}$.

6.7.2. Nouns in -ик, -ник, -чик, -щик

The suffix {-ик} forms agentive nouns, diminutives, and affectionate words. As expected for a suffix beginning with a front vowel, consonants are phonologically soft before this suffix. The following combinations do not occur: -гик, -кик, -хик, and apparently never did, since there are no instances of -жик, -чик, -шик derived from the former. Instances of the latter do not have velar counterparts:

(56) óрлик   PR "softening," loss of fleeting vowel (cf. *орёл*)

      ёжик   no alternation, associated with *ёж*

      мужи́к   no alternation, associated with *муж*

      кóвшик   no alternation, associated with *ковш*

In summary, this suffix is not involved with any morphophonemic rule with the exception the rule "fv," as indicated by the first example in (56).

The suffix {-чик} occurs only with hard consonants (except л, which is always soft when preceding this suffix). Hushers also occur with this suffix, but like those in (56), they are not associated with velars. Examples:

(57) го́лубь ~ голу́бчик   soft б́ alternates with hard б
       {го́луб′+∅} ~ {голу́б-чик+∅}
       бока́л ~ бока́льчик   hard л alternates with soft л′
       перебежа́ть ~ перебе́жчик   no alternation
       обтя́жка ~ обтя́жчик   no alternation

Nouns with the suffix {-ник} exhibit the same alternations as those with чик:

(58) весть ~ ве́стник   soft т′ alternates with hard т
       пусты́рь ~ пусты́рник   soft р′ alternates with hard р
       шко́ла ~ шко́льник   hard л alternates with soft л′
       мальчи́шка ~ мальчи́шник   no alternation
       рабо́та ~ рабо́тник   no alternation

The suffix {-щик} acts like {-ник} and {-чик}: no consonants are soft with this suffix (*фона́рь ~ фона́рщик*), except -л- (*игла́ ~ иго́льщик*). In addition, fleeting vowels are present with this suffix (*у́голь/у́гля ~ у́гольщик*). But this is expected according to the rule "fv" as given in 6.6. No velars or hushers occur with this suffix.

Practice

A. Form nouns using the suffixes given in parentheses.

1. обману́ть (+щик)   5. ходьба́ (+щик)
2. паке́т (+ик)   6. второ́й (+ник)
3. парово́з (+ник)   7. заказа́ть (+чик)
4. бесе́да (+чик)   8. мы́ло (+щик)

9. ба́ня (+щик)   11. па́мять (+ник)
10. котёл (+щик)   12. захвати́ть (+чик)

6.7.3. Nouns in *-ин, -анин (-янин), -чанин*

These suffixes represent variations of a morpheme meaning "person from" or "person of." The first variant is used in words (mostly borrowings) that already end in *-ан* (or *-ян*). The second variant relates words to place names, and the third variant occurs with roots ending in *-в*:

(59) a. пурита́нин (*puritan*)
          мусульма́нин (*mussulman*)
          лютера́нин (*Lutheran*)
          парижа́нин (*Parisian*)
          славя́нин (*славян-ский*)
          молдава́нин (*молдован-ский*)

      b. юг (*южа́нин*)
          египтя́нин (*еги́пет*)
          северя́нин (*се́вер*)
          Рижа́нин (*Ри́га*)
          Росси́я́нин (*Росси́я*)
          иркутя́нин (*Ирку́тск*)

      c. полтавча́нин
          харьковча́нин
          ростовча́нин

The variants *-ин* and *-чанин* are not associated with alternations. The variant *-анин*, however, cooccurs with soft consonants and with hushers. Since these alternations occur regularly, we are able to describe them by morphophonemic rule:

(60) MR "анин"   С, к, г, х: С′, ч, ж, ш __ {*анин}
                      (C=paired consonant)

(For *x~ш, к~ч*, see *Палéх ~ палешáнин, полк ~ полчáнин*.) This suffix is therefore marked as regularly occurring with hushers and soft-paired consonants: {*анин}. Since this is a regular alternation, the morphological transcription of a word like *северя́нин* 'northerner' is {сэвэр' -*áнин +Ø}.

Finally, note that this suffix is also involved in a number of suppletive combinations: *гóрод ~ горожáнин, Вóлогда ~ вологжáнин*. With these words, Russian speakers simply know two (or more) morphologically unrelated forms:

(61)   'town'

{гóрод-}   {горóж}~анин~   ...

6.7.4. Nouns in -к {-*/к}, {-оч}

This suffix occurs in diminutives (when related to other nouns) and resultatives (when related to verbs):

(62) бумáга ~ бумáжка   загрузи́ть ~ загру́зка
      водá ~ вóдка   обрабóтать ~ обрабóтка
      телéга ~ телéжка   вы́ставить ~ выставка
      дéньги ~ дéнежка   добáвить ~ добáвка
      стрелá ~ стрéлка   командировáть ~ командирóвка
      клеть ~ клéтка   наклáдывать ~ наклáдка
      земля́ ~ земéлька   окрáсить ~ окрáска
      корóбка ~ корóбочка   оцени́ть ~ оцéнка

It is clear from the data in (62) that no alternations occur when this suffix is concatenated with a verbal root. When connected with a nominal root, however, final velars alternate with hushers (*бумáга ~ бумáжка*), and final soft consonants (except our old friend soft *л'*) alternate with hard variants. Fleeting vowels also are present with this suffix, as expected from the rule "fv."

(63) MR "dim"   C', к, г, х : С, ч, ж, ш __ {-*/к}   (С≠л)

As indicated, we find that this suffix contains a fleeting vowel: *голóвка ~ голóвок, бумáжка ~ бумáжек, загрýзка ~ загрýзок* {голóв -*/к +а}, {бумáж -*/к +а}, {загрýз -*/к +а}. It is important to note that there is a fleeting vowel with this suffix only in inflectional terms, e.g., when it is the last suffix in the word. If a new word is derived from a stem with a fleeting vowel by adding another suffix to the end of the word, the original fleeting vowel and consonant alternations are "frozen." In the new word they are no longer inflectional alternations: *кнѝга* {книг +а}, *кнѝжка* {книж -*/к +а}, *кнѝжечка* {книж -оч -*/к +а}. This point applies to all fleeting vowels. We will only mark a suffix or root with a fleeting vowel when it is involved in inflection, when the vowel appears or disappears in different forms of that particular word. (Also see 6.7.10 and 6.7.11.)

Practice

A. Write the second word in each pair from (62) in MT.

6.7.5. Nouns in *-ние* {-*(э)ний}

The suffix {ний} is found in abstract neuter nouns that are related to 1st conj **verb** roots ending in a vowel. If the verb stem ends in a consonant ({нэс-}, {тэк-}, etc.) then a filler vowel {э} is added between the consonant and this suffix: *несéние, течéние*, etc. This filler vowel occurs with soft consonants phonologically and with hushers morphophonemically. When the suffix {-ний} is added to a stem ending in a vowel there are no alternations, except for shift of stress. Examples follow.

(64)	опоздá(ть)	~	опоздáние	
	поругá(ть)	~	поругáние	
	воздержá(ть)	~	воздержáние	
	спас(тѝ)	~	спасéние	{спас -*э́ний +о}
	текý	~	течéние	{тэч -*э́ний +о}

When this suffix occurs with verb roots found in 2nd conj verbs, the same filler vowel {э} is added to the suffix and we encounter **the same**

alternations with this suffix as we see in the *я* form of the verb. Compare:

(65) тормози́ть ~ торможу́ ~ торможе́ние (з~ж)
      относи́ть ~ отношу́ ~ отноше́ние (с~ш)
      укрепи́ть ~ укреплю́ ~ укрепле́ние (п~пл)
      сгусти́ть ~ сгущу́ ~ сгуще́ние (ст~щ)

These alternations must be suppletive, since they cannot be explained by means of a phonological rule or a morphophonemic rule (cf. *спасе́ние, ургрызе́ние*). We just analyze these words as being independent of each other. But still, there seems to be something going on, some kind of regularity with these pairs of words. What information is needed to explain the *з~ж* alternation in *тормози́ть* and *торможе́ние*?

6.7.6. Nouns in -*ок*, -*ёк*, -*ек*, -*о́нок* {-*/к)}, {-*он/к}

Velars do not occur with these suffixes, the first three of which are morphophonemically {-*/к}, the final suffix being {-*он/к}. Instead hushers occur: *снежо́к, овра́жек, скачо́к, смешо́к, казачо́нок*. Similarly, only soft consonants occur with the suffix {-*он/к} and fleeting vowels are predictable: *кит ~ китёнок, козёл ~ козлёнок*.

Practice

A. Using the suffixes provided write words that are related to the following:

1. знать	'know'	{-*(э)ний}
2. кот	'cat'	{-*о́н/к}
3. ввести́	'introduce'	{-*(э)ний}
4. цыга́н	'gypsy'	{-*о́н/к}
5. расти́	'grow'	{-*(э)ний}
6. пасту́х	'shepherd'	{-*о́н/к}
7. друг	'friend'	{-*/'к}
8. упусти́ть	'let slip'	{-*(э)ний}
9. учи́ть	'teach'	{-*(э)ний}
10. со́кол	'falcon'	{-*о́н/к}

11. чёлн	'boat'	{-*/'к}
12. бýйвол	'buffalo'	{-*óн/к}
13. назвáть	'name'	{-*(э)ний}
14. наказáть	'punish'	{-*(э)ний}
15. изложúть	'expound'	{-*(э)ний}
16. укрепúть	'strengthen'	{-*(э)ний}
17. трястú	'shake'	{-*(э)ний}
18. согласúться	'agree'	{-*(э)ний}
19. чертúть	'draw'	{-*(э)ний}
20. шум	'noise'	{-*/'к}
21. отравúть	'poison'	{-*(э)ний}
22. лисá	'fox'	{-*óн/к}
23. собáка	'dog'	{-*óн/к}
24. удвóить	'double'	{-*(э)ний}

6.7.7. Nouns in -ость {-ост'}

This suffix is found in abstract nouns related to adjectives. No alternations are observed in derivation with this suffix: *рáдость, блáгость, гúбкость*. It is not "responsible" for root final hushers: *похóжесть ~ похóжий, тя́жесть ~ тя́жкий*. Forms in -ность are derived from adjectives in -н-, as *актúвность ~ актúвный*.

6.7.8. Nouns in -ство {-(*э)ств}

Velar stems alternate with hushers; a filler vowel {*э} follows hushers: *рáбство* {раб -ств +о}, *схóдство, божествó* {бож -*эств +о}, *мýжество, кня́жество, отéчество, чудáчество*. In addition, soft consonants (except soft л) do not occur with this suffix: *звéрь ~ звéрство, издáтель ~ издáтельство*.

6.7.9. Nouns in -тель {-(*и)тэл'}

No alternations occur other than expected with the verbal suffix -и- (see your answer to Practice Exercise B in 6.5.7). This suffix occurs fused with verbal suffixes in agentive nouns: *нагреватель, свидетель, учитель* {уч -*й +т'} {уч -*йтэл' +Ø}.

Practice

A. Using the suffix in parentheses, write what noun is related to the words given below. Be ready to write each word in morphophonemic transcription.

1. вдова {*/ц}
2. глаз {*/к}
3. гриб {*/к}
4. Рига {анин}
5. чертёж {ик}
6. заготовить {*(э)ний}
7. обогревать {тэл'}
8. колокол {чик}
9. ёлка {*/к(а)}
10. бес {*óн/к}
11. бедный {ост'}
12. камень {щик}
13. зверь {*óн/к}
14. могила {*щик}
15. оговорить {*щик}

16. осёл {*óн/к}
17. кружить {*(э)ний}
18. опасный {ост'}
19. немой {*/ц}
20. подруга {*/к(а)}
21. огонь {*/к}
22. голландия {*/ц}
23. затея {*ник}
24. творить {*(э)ний}
25. книжный {ост'}
26. сапог {*ник}
27. галка {*/к(а)}
28. дружный {ост'}
29. штук {*/к(а)}
30. критика {Ø suffix}

B. What's odd about the pair *огонь ~ огонёк*?

6.7.10. Adjectives in -*н* {-*/н}*

This is one of the most productive suffixes in Russian. As expected for a consonantal suffix, fleeting vowels are present with it (*суточный*). Velars alternate with hushers and *л* is soft: *язычный, школьный*. Otherwise consonants are hard with this suffix: *грязный, словарный*. This suffix also appears as {н} with no fleeting vowel in secondary derivations. Remember that, as far as derivational morphology is concerned, a fleeting vowel can only occur in a prefix, at the end of an underived root, or as part of the final suffix in a stem. (See 6.7.4.)

(66)	шко́льный	{шко́л' -*/н +ый}
	язы́чный	{йазы́ч -*/н +ый}
	гря́зный	{гр'а́з -*/н +ый}
	земе́льный	{зэмэ́л' - */н +ый}

6.7.11. Adjectives in -ск(ий) {-(*э)ск}

This is another widely used suffix. Velars rarely occur with this suffix, instead the corresponding husher is found followed by the filler vowel {э}: *челове́ческий, куби́ческий, педогоги́ческий, бо́жеский, дру́жеский, мона́шеский.* Soft consonants (except soft л) do not occur with this suffix: *апте́карский, ца́рский, де́тский, чита́тельский, а́нгельский, се́льский.* As with other consonantal suffixes, fleeting vowels are present: *неме́цкий* {нэмэ́ц -ск +ый}.

Practice

A. What nouns pair with the following adjectives?

1. нау́чный	4. во́дочный	7. оши́бочный
2. коне́чный	5. де́нежный	8. автомоби́льный
3. ство́льный	6. оте́ческий	9. биологи́ческий

B. What adjectives with suffix {-*/н} are related to the following?

1. ме́сто	4. грусть	7. культу́ра	10. доро́га
2. успе́х	5. ме́сяц	8. семья́	11. мы́ло
3. грех	6. тетра́дка	9. вкус	12. ружьё

6.8. Summing Up

Pronunciation rules seem to have a life cycle of their own. They come into existence hesitantly in rapid speech and colloquial usage and as characteristics of dialectal speech. They may then become fully operative throughout most of the language as full-fledged phonological processes. Then new sound changes may occur that restrict and ultimately stop the previous process. Often a trace of earlier sound shifts can be seen as "irregularities" in the language. We account for some of these irregularities by means of morphophonemic rules.

Modern Russian has fleeting vowels and alternations in inflected words and in pairs of words related to each other through suffixation. When confronted with these alternations most well-educated Russian speakers say that these are simply exceptional forms which must be learned. While this is true of suppletive relationships, morphophonemics shows us that some of these "exceptions" often occur in restricted and definable situations. Fleeting vowels are not expected just anywhere: some morphemes are expected to have fleeting vowels and the rule "fv" describes which fleeting vowel will occur. Morphophonemics allows us to **describe** many of the alternations whose presence in the modern language is due to ancient sound changes but that are no longer productive. Now that we have described the variations that exist, we know the "what." We are now ready to ask and answer the question, "Why does Russian have these alternations?" To answer the question "why," we will have to look back into the history of Russian to find out what happened that brought about the situation we find today.

Part III

Historical Sound Changes

CHAPTER 7

7.1. Why Study the History of Russian

Up to now we have been describing modern Russian, and in particular, many of the alternations in sound and endings that can make learning Russian complex. We have postponed asking "why" questions in favor of asking "what" and "how" is Russian put together. In this chapter we will address the why questions. Why does Russian have alternations? Why does it have fleeting vowels? Why is *e* sometimes *é* and sometimes *ë*? Why doesn't the writing match what is spoken all the time? Why do different morphemes have the same meaning, such as {град-} 'city' and {город-} 'city'? It is only by understanding the changes that occurred in the language in centuries and millennia past that we can understand why the variations we have studied exist today. Our rules are valuable for describing the language, but now we must examine why these rules developed. This is not simply an exercise in curiosity: once the reasons behind the rules are understood, it is often easier to remember them and to know where to expect them.

Languages change over time. Words are borrowed into a language and other words "die out" for lack of use. Words can acquire new meanings. Even pronunciation changes, sometimes radically, over the centuries. For example, even native English speakers can't understand Old English without extensive study of its forms and vocabulary. It is sometimes difficult for speakers of American English to understand speakers of British English although both languages derive from a common ancestor. Evidence of language change can come from written records, from comparing related languages, and from information obtained by comparing a language against itself, including dialectal data. Eastern Slavic people, the ancestors of the Russians, have been

НАШИ ПРЕДКИ.

ДАВНО, давно въ странѣ, гдѣ мы теперь живемъ, не было ни богатыхъ городовъ, ни каменныхъ домовъ, ни большихъ селъ. Были одни только поля, да густые темные лѣса, въ которыхъ жили дикіе звѣри.

По берегамъ рѣкъ, далеко другъ отъ друга стояли бѣдныя избушки. Въ избушкахъ жили наши предки—славяне, такъ назывался тогда русскій народъ.

Славяне были храбрымъ народомъ. Они много воевали со своими сосѣдями и часто ходили на охоту, чтобы убивать дикихъ звѣрей, которые выбѣгали изъ лѣсовъ и нападали на людей.

writing for nearly a thousand years. What hints regarding the makeup of modern Russian can we get by looking at earlier written records?

7.2. The Alphabet of Bygone Years

If you look at a book or newspaper printed in Russia before 1917 you will immediately notice that there are certain differences in the way Russian used to be written. Consider, for example, "Наши предки," on the opposite page. This page is from a history book for children published about 1912 in St. Petersburg. A speaker from the early twentieth century reading this text would sound much like a modern Russian speaker. In other words, the text is not a phonetic representation of how the words were spoken.

We know this from descriptions of Russian published at that time and from the speech of Russians who were alive at the beginning of the 20th century. It is not surprising that spelling and speech do not always match. Writing often tends to be representative of how a language was spoken at an earlier time. While language continues to change, the way it is written becomes fixed in print and the written forms change very slowly. Thus the English *night* and *know* are not pronounced the way they are spelled. The spelling of these words represents a much older pronunciation which has been lost. In Russia, it took a major social revolution to change its standardized spelling.

Following the 1917 revolution orthographic changes were made so that written Russian matched its pronunciation more closely. In particular, several letters were either dropped from the language or replaced.

Practice

A. Be ready to "translate" into modern Russian the text "Наши предки."

B. The writing in "Наши предки," although easily recognizable and readable, is somewhat different from what we are used to today. The differences can be classified into two types: (1) letters that are no longer used in Russian, and (2) letters that are still used but used differently. Read through "Наши предки" and determine which letters belong to each group.

C. What modern Russian letters correspond to *ѣ* (ѣ) and *i*?

D. Do you see anything surprising about the use of the letter ъ in "На́ши пре́дки"?

E. Where does the letter *i* turn up in "На́ши пре́дки"?

7.2.1. *e* vs. ѣ

In modern Russian, there are really two kinds of *e*. One represents the sound [o] (orthographic *ё*) when under stress. The other represents [э] when under stress. This difference can be seen in: *нес* (*нёс*), *снег*.

In modern Russian we find [э] alternating with [o] in related morphemes: *пче́льник* {пчэ́л'-*ник +Ø} *пчёлы* {пчо́л +ы}, both with a root meaning 'bee.' There is no rule that relates these two roots—they must be learned separately. However, the reason for this alternation can be easily understood from a historical perspective. Before the twelfth century Old Russian only had one -*e*- (and no -*ё*-), usually written as ε in the oldest texts. Sometime between the twelfth and fourteenth centuries a shift in pronunciation occurred: the sound [э] **under stress and before a hard consonant** began to be pronounced as [o]. We could write this as a historical phonological rule:

(1)   э~o rule   э́ → о́C   (C=hard consonant)

The rule in (1) states that the sound [э] shifted to [o] when it was stressed **and** located before a hard consonant. We will discuss why this change happened in the next section. After the fourteenth century we have a new [o], but it was still spelled *e*.

> Изменение [э] в [o] происходило в положении после мягких согласных перед твердым, причем при таком изменении мягкость предшествующего согласного сохранялось.
>
> (Иванов)

This historical sound change allows us to trace the history of *пчёлы* and see why *пче́льник* does not have a -*ё*-:

(2) Proto-Slavic   пчѐлы   пчѐльникъ

    AD 1200–1400

    (э → о)   пч[о]лы   no change

    1700   пчёлы   пчѐльникъ   (spelling innovations)

There is no -*ё*- in *пчѐльник* because the stressed [э] fell before a soft consonant.

This explains why we have the [э] ~ [о] alternation as in *нести* ~ *нёс*, and most other words with -*ё*-. If -*ё*- comes from an earlier [э], spelled є or *e*, why don't we just use [э] in our description of modern Russian and include the rule in (1)? This would be easy and would allow us to avoid using odd morphemes such as {*o}. Two reasons.

First, while it is theoretically **possible** that whenever Russians say *нёс*, they first start off with *нес* and then apply the rule in (1) to get *нёс*, we believe that this is unlikely. Instead the rule in (1), though historically accurate, plays no role in modern Russian. Speakers simply know [н'ос] is the past tense masc of *нести*.

Second, there really isn't anything odd about {*o}. This is simply a symbol for an [o] that is preceded by a soft consonant. And we want to write an [o], instead of *ё*, because of our desire to have one sound – one symbol. But, even if we insist that there is something odd about {*o}, there is the undeniable problem that the rule in (1) is no longer active in the modern language. There are many words that show this, *нет*, *снег*, and *мѐсто* being just three. No one says *нёт*, *снёг*, *мёсто*. Why not? Why didn't the rule in (1) apply to these words too?

The writing in "Нáши прéдки" gives us a hint about why *снег*, *нет*, *мѐсто* and other words did not undergo the shift of [э] → [o]. Read the first three lines of "Нáши прéдки" out loud. Which letter in the text equates to modern *ё*?

An older stage of Russian contained the vowels *e* and *ѣ*[1]. The letter *ѣ* is called "yat'" (*ятъ*). It became *e* in modern Russian. It did not become *ё*. Russian dictionaries published before the twentieth century give, for example, *снѣгъ*. On the other hand, original *e* when under stress and before a hard consonant corresponds perfectly with modern Russian *ё*; cf. in "Нáши прéдки": *живемъ*, *селъ*, *темные*. The *e* in words like *теперь* does not correspond to modern Russian *ё* because it

---

[1] This is the symbol for yat (ѣ) in italics.

is not under stress, or if it is under stress it does not fall before a hard consonant (cf. also *берегáмъ, людéй*). Note that the word *прéдки* is borrowed from South Slavic, which did not have the [э] → [o] sound change as described above, the Russian root being ПЕРЕД- (cf. Russian *вперёд*).

We conclude that words such as *нет, снег, мéсто* do not have a *ё* because at an earlier stage they didn't have the sound [э] (which changed to [o]) but a different sound, namely *ѣ*. Sometime before the latter sound shifted to *e*, the sound shift expressed in (1) ceased to operate in Russian:

(3)	Proto-Slavic		*живéтъ	снѣгъ
	e → o	(ca. AD 1200)	живётъ	———
	ѣ → e	(ca. AD 1300)	———	снегъ

Practice

A.   How would the following words have been **written** before 1917?

1. нет (remember final -ъ)
2. мéсто
3. мёд
4. берёза
5. рекá (gen pl рек)

6. нестú (past masc: нёс)
7. стенá (nom pl стéны)
8. сесть (он сел)
9. женá (nom pl жёны)
10. смех

7.2.2. The Pronunciation of ѣ

Recall that Old Russian -*e*, also spelled *є*, under stress and before a hard consonant yielded modern Russian -*ё*: *берéза* → *берёза*. Old Russian yat' (*ѣ*) yielded modern Russian -*e*: *снѣгъ* → *снег*. How did the pronunciation of *ѣ* differ from *e* in Old Russian? Since all instances of *ѣ* have shifted to *e* in Russian, we must consult closely related languages, namely other Slavic languages, which may have had—or perhaps still have—a sound corresponding to *ѣ*. By comparing words that have this letter with similar words in other Slavic languages we try to get an approximation of what sound this letter represented.

Consider the words in (4). The Russian forms all have the stressed vowel *e*, that is, they go back to words that had the vowel *ѣ*. (Note the *j* in Serbian is pronounced much like [й].)

(4) | **Russian** | **Ukrainian** | **Polish** | **Serb** | **Bulg** |
| --- | --- | --- | --- | --- |
| лес | ліс | las | лијес | лес |
| снег | сніг | śnieg | снијег | сняг |
| мéсто | місто | miasto | мјесто | място |
| бéлый | білий | biały | бијела | бял |

A comparison of Russian and Ukrainian consistently shows two different modern pronunciations for Old Russian *ѣ*: *e* in Russian and *i* in Ukrainian. Polish shows a diphthong (*ie* or *ia*) in three of its forms and diphthongs are prominent in the Serbian forms, while Bulgarian consistently gives *я*. Thus:

(5) | | *ѣ* |
| --- | --- |
| Russian | e |
| Ukrainian | i |
| Polish | ia, ie, a |
| SCr | ије, је |
| Bulgarian | я, е |

The comparative method provides a variety of sounds to choose from as representing the pronunciation of *ѣ*. But certain tendencies surface. Judging from the data given above, *ѣ* must have been a front vowel. We know that it was not [э], since this pronunciation attends another letter, *e*, and since [э] shifted to [o], whereas *ѣ* did not. Another possibility is that *ѣ* was pronounced as the front vowel [и], but [и] does not shift to [э], cf. Old Russian *говори́тъ* ~ Modern Russian *говори́т*. Other comparative data suggest either a diphthong [ia] or [ie] or, according to Bulgarian a front vowel like [æ], as in English *ca̱t*.

The fact that Russian words with yat' were borrowed into Finnish usually with a long [æ] or a diphthong supports the proposition that Old Russian *ѣ* was pronounced as [æ] or as a diphthong [iæ]. Examples from Finnish (where -ä- [æ]: *määrä* < *мѣ̱ра* 'measure', *läävä* < *хлѣ̱въ* 'cattle shed'.

Practice

A. There ought to be some dialectal evidence of the pronunciation of old *ѣ*. Read through the following transcription of an 83-year old speaker from the village of *Разгоняй* in the *Солигаличский* region. It is from "Хрестомáтия по рýсской диалектолóгии." We have provided a gloss for obscure words.

B. What generally is the following text about?

Солигаличский район, дер. Разгоняй

45. Пошлá за йáгодам // нáт'е-ка тýт ц'ерн'и́ц'ина / а тýт брусн'и́-ц'ина / а боров'и́к-то это гр'ип //

и зд'и́с'а л'он д'е́лал'и / т'ер'еб'и́л'и / а кáк дожы́ идýт/ так в'áжом срáзу и в бáпк'и // а потóм из р'и́г'и на сушы́уку / а колды́ дóма слáл'и / д'е́лал'и шéрс' / хоýйсты ткáл'и //

Н'иц'евó н'и́ету / до гóрода п'ешéц'ком / з'имóй на салáсках / лáпотк'и д'ие́лал'и / лы́ко мужы́к'и д'иелáл'и / онýц'к'и б'ие́лыйе да св'и́ету б'ие́лова н'е в'и́д'иш / выхóд'ит тáк жылá //

Медв'и́д'и / воýк'и / л'и́сы таскáйут кýр'иц нáц'исто // мáт' фе'ó зд'и́с'а в'éрт'ица / б'éгайот в'езд'и́ //

у нáс н'и́ет рáйсково л'и́ето / н'ед'и́л'а пров'ерн'óца / тýт оп'éт' с'и́в'ер / нóн'ц'е-то полов'и́к'й ткáл'и/ оп'éт' крáс'ила ф ц'угунк'é / йéт'и фс'ó сóс'енк'и сод'и́л'и / в нац'áл'е колхóза сóтн'и йáблон'ей былó //

по гр'и́бы йа ход'и́ла // мáсл'ен'ик'и сушý / а йéт'и ф ц'ýгун и ф п'éц'ку //

1981 г., Залеткина К. П., 83 года, неграмотная.

нате-ка – there you have	саласки – toboggan, sleigh
церницина – billberry	лапотки – bast shoes
брусницина – red whortleberry	лыко – bast bark
боровик – edible mushroom	онуцки – cloth socks worn in bast shoes
лён – flax	нацисто = начисто 'openly'
теребить – pull (flax)	сивер = север 'холод'
вязать – bind, tie	нонце-то – now
бабка – shock, bunch	половик – floor mat
рига – threshing barn	цугунка – cast iron stove
колды = когда	сосенки – pine trees
шерсь = шерсть	

C. Find four words that used to have a *ѣ*. How are they transcribed in this dialect?

D. How does this dialect support the argument that *ѣ* used to be a diphthong?

7.2.3. Front and Back Jers

Another plain difference that can be seen in "На́ши пре́дки" is the presence of a "hard sign" (ъ) at the end of many words, as in *богатыхъ*, where in modern Russian there is no hard sign. Thus all words in the text "На́ши пре́дки" end in a vowel, *й*, *ь*, or *ъ*. The preponderance of vowels at word final position suggests that at some earlier time in Russian the hard sign and soft sign were also vowels. A quick check of Bulgarian, where *ъ* is still pronounced, confirms this suggestion: compare Bulg. *сън, църква* ~ Russ. *сон, це́рковь*. In Old Russian, the hard sign is called a "back jer" (*ер*) and the soft sign is called a "front jer" (*ерь*). These are also called "reduced" or "weak" vowels. Back jers are found in words whose modern counterparts do not contain hard signs. Compare words from "На́ши пре́дки":

(6)	**Older Russian**	**Modern Russian**
	въ	в
	городовъ	городо́в
	селъ	сёл
	рѣкъ	рек
	народомъ	наро́дом

The letter *ъ* has not survived at the end of words in modern Russian. The front jer, however, continues as a "soft sign" in basically the same position it occupied in older Russian texts: *тепе́рь*, for example, although it is no longer pronounced. At the end of words *ъ* has been lost altogether. However, the sign *ь* has ingeniously been retained to **show** that the consonant preceding it is pronounced soft. For this reason we can propose that this jer must have been a front vowel capable of causing softening of consonants, like the other front vowels *и*, *e*, and *ѣ*. Conversely, we are safe in assuming that *ъ* was a back vowel: no soft consonants occur in modern Russian where a *ъ* followed. Here is how V. V. Ivanov characterized the pronunciation of jers in Old Russian:

В древнерусском языке были две гласные фонемы непол-
ного образования, так называемые редуцированные или
глухие. Это были ослабленные гласные, произносившиеся,
вероятно, неполным голосом. Условно эти гласные обозна-
чаются [ъ] (ер) и [ь] (ерь). Гласная фонема [ъ] характеризо-
валась признаками непереднего ряда среднего подъема, а
[ь]—переднего ряда среднего подъема.

Ivanov describes both jers as reduced vowels. He characterizes ъ as a
nonfront mid vowel and ь as a front mid vowel. The letter ъ at one
time was pronounced as a reduced "uh" sound as the *o* in the word
"p̲o̲lite," and the letter ь was pronounced as a reduced "ih" sound as
the *i* in the word "mass̲i̲ve." Try reading aloud the words in the left
column in (6), giving proper pronunciation to the jers.

As indicated above, the actual pronunciation of jers at word final
position has been lost in modern Russian. Traces of front jers remain in
the softness of consonants:

(7)   Old Russ.: тепé[р'ь] → final jer lost → Modern Russian тепé[р']

A trace of the front jer is present in the soft quality of the final consonant. The writing in "Нáши прéдки" shows an earlier stage of Russian had an enriched vowel system, containing at least three more
vowel letters (ъ, ь, and ѣ) than are found in the modern language. The
presence of these vowels helps to explain why consonants are soft before soft signs: soft signs used to be front vowels. In addition, it provides clues to the question of why the *e* in *снѣг* does not shift to *ё* (earlier it was not a *e*, but a ѣ).

Before we dig deeper into the history of Russian in our search to
understand why the language is the way it is, we should answer one
question that may be bothering the reader. Why does language change
at all, and in particular, why did Old Russian *é* shift to *ё*?

7.2.4. Why [э] → [o]?

When sound changes occur across a given language, it is usually because speakers have found it more convenient to speak in the new
way. This is not necessarily a matter of laziness, but more of efficiency
of expression. As we have already seen, "simplification" in one area of

the language often results in a new complexity in another part of the language. For example, the shift of *ѣ* to *e* resulted in a simplification in the language (fewer sounds), but this, in turn, triggered the development of a new morphophonemic rule involving {*o}.

Sound changes often involve **assimilation**, where one sound becomes more like the sound next to it. We have seen assimilation in the modern language; words such as *прόсьба* [прόз'бъ] show assimilation of the feature "voice." Though the root in the related *просúть* contains a voiceless [c], the derived noun contains its voiced counterpart. Assimilation makes speech easier and more efficient.

We have seen that the Old Russian *é* shifted to *ё* ([o]) when before a hard consonant (cf. *смéртъ* ~ *мёртвый*). Recall that vowels can be mapped according to where they are produced in the mouth. Thus [и] is a high front vowel (the tongue is raised and approaches the front ridge of the mouth) and can be charted so with the other vowels:

(8)	front	back
high	и	ы у
mid	э	o
low		a

By using binary markings (+ and – for each articulatory feature) we can define each sound in terms of all its features, as shown in (9).

(9)	[и]
high	+
low	–
front	+
rounded	–

The feature "rounded" refers to whether or not the lips are rounded in pronunciation of the vowel. It is needed to distinguish between [ы] and [y]. Mid vowels, namely [э] and [o], are characterized as being neither high nor low, i.e., [–high, –low]. Similarly, we don't need to use the term "back" because a sound that is [+front] is by default [–back] and one that is [–front] is automatically [+back].

We can now assign binary markings to all the vowels in (8):

(10)	и	э	у	ы	о	а
high	+	–	+	+	–	–
low	–	–	–	–	–	+
front	+	+	–	–	–	–
rounded	–	–	+	–	+	–

Notice that all vowels are characterized differently. The only difference between [ы] and [у] is that the former is marked [–rounded]. In Russian, the feature [+rounded] is generally only used to distinguish between these two sounds. It is redundant for [o], since no other vowel is characterized [–high, –low, –front].

Redundancies occur with some of the other sounds as well. For example, we can define the sound [и] by means of all the features given above, but there is only one vowel that is [+high, +front], namely [и]. The other features ([–low] [–rounded]) are all redundant for [и].

Practice

A. What vowel(s) is/are:

1. [+high, +front]   4. [–high, +front]
2. [–high, –low]   5. [–high, –front]
3. [+front, +low]   6. [+rounded]

B. Without using the feature [rounded], what are the nonredundant (defining) features for:

1. [ə]   2. [o]

C. In which feature do [ə] and [o] differ?

By using binary features historical phonological rules are written to express actual changes in articulation. For example, if we wanted to say that the sound [ə] shifts to [o] in some circumstance, we could write:

(11) ə → o / ___ X   (where X = some sound)

But what is really happening in this sound change is a change in articulation, namely:

(12)   [–high, +front] → [–front] / _____ X

The rule in (12) states that any vowel that is [–high, +front] (there is only one, namely [ə]) shifts to a vowel that is [–high, –front] in the environment of X. That is to say, the only change is the feature [+front] shifts to [–front]. Any sound that is [–high] and [+front] becomes [–front]. Schematically, with salient features in italics:

(13)   **[ə]**   →   **[o]**

–high	*–high*	(no change)
–low	–low	(no change)
+front	*–front*	(changed by rule in 5)
–round	+round	(automatic)

Remember that the feature [+rounded] is redundant (automatic) for [o], so it need not be specified in the rule. So, while it may seem like a distinct and major change, the actual shift of [ə] to [o] really involves just one small shift in articulation, namely the shift of [+front] to [–front]. Why should such a shift occur? Why weren't Old Russians satisfied with saying [ə] when it was under stress before a hard consonant? Why did they start pronouncing this vowel as [o]?

Here is the inventory of vowel sounds in Russian at the time of the change of [ə] to [o].

(14)

	front	**back**
high	и	ы у
mid	ѣ є	о
low		а

When a sound change occurs it often involves the shift of only one feature.

Practice

D. What feature shift occurred when [ə] shifted to [o]?

E. Why should this shift occur? (Hint: Recall that in the pronunciation of hard consonants, the body of the tongue is [–high, –front] in comparison to soft counterparts.)

7.3. Linguistic Relatives

In the preceding sections Russian, or an older variant of Russian, was compared to other Slavic languages in order to arrive at an approximation of how ѣ may have been pronounced. We did not try to find commonalities with non-Slavic languages, such as Chinese or Hopi, an American Indian language, because research has shown that these languages have very little in common with Russian. It has been shown, however, that many languages spoken in Central and Eastern Europe share many features, particularly in word roots and grammar. Russian, Ukrainian, and Belorussian are particularly close and compose a language group, the East Slavic languages. They are close because they largely derive from a single source.

Russian derives from Early Russian or Old Russian (OR), which was an eastern dialect of late Common Slavic (общеславянский), an ancient language which died out (=evolved out) about one thousand years ago. It is the basis of three language groups that form today's Slavic languages. Common Slavic itself comes from Proto-Slavic (праславянский)—the earliest Slavic dialect of the mother language, Indo-European. Listed in (15) are the principal modern West, South, and East Slavic languages. There are no written records of either Common Slavic or Proto Slavic, but by means of internal reconstruction and the comparative method, they have been reconstructed to a certain degree. The table in (15) indicates main genetic relationships only and does not indicate relative chronology for the formation of the languages involved.

The first writing in Slavic is in so-called Old Church Slavic (OCS), a South Slavic dialect of late Common Slavic, though some OCS writings have eastern (Old Russian) characteristics. This leads to the suggestion that OR and OCS were simply two variants of late Common Slavic. In any event, it is not surprising that a southern Slavic variant of writing should be adopted in Old Rus' since the Greek church spread its influence, including writing, via the South Slavic lands.

(15)

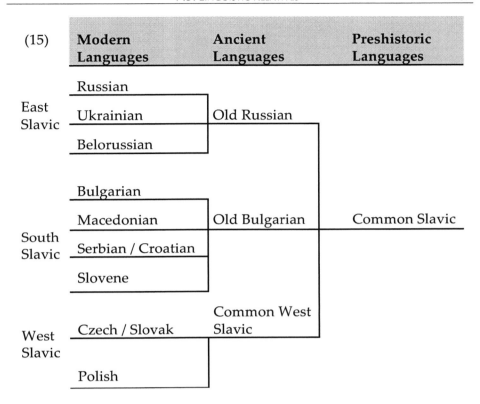

Modern Languages		Ancient Languages	Preshistoric Languages
	Russian		
East Slavic	Ukrainian	Old Russian	
	Belorussian		
	Bulgarian		
South Slavic	Macedonian	Old Bulgarian	Common Slavic
	Serbian / Croatian		
	Slovene		
West Slavic	Czech / Slovak	Common West Slavic	
	Polish		

Sister languages to Common Slavic include Germanic (a source of English), Celtic, Hindi, Armenian, Greek, the Romance group (French, Italian, Spanish, etc.), Albanian, Persian, and the Baltic group (Lithuanian, Latvian, Old Prussian).

The Slavic languages, while dissimilar enough to be separate languages, have similar words and grammar. One interesting aspect of Russian is the presence of numerous words with the combination *оло, оро,* and *ере* in the root: *хóлод, гóрод, бéрег,* for example. Yet these roots appear in an abbreviated form in other words *хладнокрóвный* 'cool, composed,' *градострóитель* 'town planner,' *безбрéжный* 'boundless.' The roots of these words (ХЛАД-, ГРАД-, and БРЕГ-) are historically related to *хóлод, гóрод,* and *бéрег,* that is each pair (i.e., *город-* and *град-*) goes back to one word or root. It is difficult to determine from Russian alone which variant is historically derived from the other: the one filled out with vowels, such as *город,* or the one with only one vowel, *град.* Or perhaps they both go back to some form now not present in the modern language. Historical documents could certainly help resolve this problem, if only we had documents written in early Common Slavic, but we may also resolve this question by means of the comparative method: similar words in closely related languages can be compared. Then a decision can be made regarding an earlier stage of the words, when the compared languages were one. The decision must take into account as much information as is available. Consider, for example, the pairs of words given in (16).

(16)

Russian	Bulgarian	S-Croat	Polish	Czech	OCS
го́лос	глас	глас	głos	hlas	гласъ
го́род	град	град	gród	hrad	градъ
голова́	глава	глава	głowa	hlava	глава
во́лос	власи	влас	włos	vlas	власъ
бе́рег	брег	бриjег	brzeg	břeh	брѣгъ
берёза	бреза	бреза	brzoza	bříza	not cited
борода́	брада	брада	broda	brada	брада
де́рево	дърво	дриjево	drzewo	dřevo	дрѣво
зо́лото	злато	злато	złoto	zlato	злато
молоко́	мляко	млиjеко	mleko	mleko	млѣко

Words with the sequence illustrated in (16) are usually called "TORT forms" in Slavic, where T=any consonant, O=the vowel *o* or *e*, and R=one of the sonorants *p* or *л*. As shown in (16) TORT forms in Russian are generally fully voiced, that is, they are TOROT forms. In Russian this is called *полногла́сие* (full voicing).

Practice

A. Judging by the data in (16), which sequence is represented most in the Slavic languages: TORT, TOROT, or TROT?

B. Of the languages which have TROT, which consistently have the vowel *a* and which have the vowel *o*?

C. Based on your answers above, what form, TORT, TOROT, or TROT appears to have been used in the Common Slavic?

In spite of the numerical preponderance of TROT (or TRAT) forms in the modern languages it is generally believed that these words in Common Slavic had the form TORT and that the shift to TROT and TOROT took place in a late stage of Common Slavic, when the latter was breaking up. This view is supported by evidence of obsolete words from various Slavic languages: Russ *запортак* 'dried out egg' cf. Russ *запороток*; Medieval Bulg *балтина* 'swamp,' *малдичие* 'youth,' *залтарин* 'gold smith,' Polabian *storna* 'side,' *morz* 'frost,' *korvo* 'cow.' Old records from northern Polish have *karw* 'bullock' and place names such as *Wyszegard*. Around the middle of the 9th century Common Slavic TORT forms began shifting into the forms we see today. A Byzantine text written previous to 860 AD has the name *Valdimer*, and the earliest loan words into Finnish do not show the shift: Finnish *palttina* 'linen', *talkkuna* 'oatmeal', *taltta* 'chisel', and *värttinä* 'spindle'; cf. Russian *полотно́, молокно́, долото́, веретено́*. These data provide evidence for the belief that these words in Common Slavic had the form TORT.

A non-Slavic language which has many correspondences with Slavic is Lithuanian, an Indo-European language spoken in the Baltic region, neighboring the Slavic area. In (17) we compare the TOROT forms given above with their Lithuanian counterparts. We are particularly interested in the shape of the stem in Lithuanian: will it be TORT, TOROT, or TROT? (Note: the nom sg ending for masc nouns in Lithuanian is *-as* or *-us*.) There is no clear Lithuanian counterpart for *бе́рег*.

(17)	a.	го́лос	balsas	'voice'
	b.	го́род	gardas	'fold, pen'
	c.	молоко́	malkas	'draught'
	d.	во́лос	vilna	'wool'
	e.	зо́лото	geltonas	'yellow'
	f.	голова́	galva	'head'
	g.	бе́рег	——	'shore'
	h.	берёза	beržas	'birch'

(17) i. борода́   barzda   'beard'

      j. де́рево   derva   'resin, pitch'

Note that Lithuanian, a language which has changed little over the millenia, has the sequence TORT. In this regard it is interesting to note the English correspondences to these words (none for *голова́*).

(18) a. го́лос   'call'   f. голова́   ———

      b. го́род   'yard'   g. бе́рег   'park/burg'

      c. молоко́   'milk'   h. берёза   'birch'

      d. во́лос   'wool'   i. борода́   'beard'

      e. зо́лото   'gold'   j. де́рево   'tree'

We may make the following summations. The Slavic languages present different root sequences for roots with the sonorants *р* and *л*: TOROT (East Slavic), TROT, and TRAT (West and South Slavic). Other Indo-European languages (notably Lithuanian and Germanic) present the sequence: TORT. For this reason TORT is considered the older form, TOROT and TROT are innovations in Slavic.

If TOROT forms are normal for Russian, why do TROT and TRAT variants also occur in Russian? Speakers of Old Russian were likely influenced by the language used in religious settings, Old Church Slavic. Old Church Slavic, like other south Slavic languages did not undergo full voicing, and is the source of the second form in pairs such as *го́род* and -*град*, *хо́лод* and -*хлад* in Russian. These are borrowings into Russian. They are not considered unusual by modern speakers of Russian, just as most speakers of modern English don't think about the historical source of words such as *beef, mirror,* or *cemetery* (all from French), even though English has retained the Anglo-Saxon words: *cow, looking glass, graveyard.*

The comparison of words with the sequence TOROT explains why Russian has dual forms such as *го́род* and -*град*. This comparison shows there is a consistent relationship between Russian and other Indo-European languages and particularly with South Slavic. In the next section, we'll look more closely at how OCS became the literary language—the language of writing—in places like Novgorod, Kiev, and Moscow.

7.3.1. Missionary Brothers

In the ninth century the Slavic peoples had, for the most part, migrated to their present locations. Although they were geographically dispersed, the dialects that they spoke were quite similar to each other, much closer than they are today. It should also be noted that most of the Slavic peoples at this time had not yet converted to Christianity. The Russians did not officially accept Christianity until the end of the tenth century.

Ninth-century fresco of St. Cyril in the Basilica di San Clement, Rome

In the mid ninth century, somewhere near the modern-day Czech Republic, a new Slavic empire known as Moravia the Great was taking shape. For political and religious reasons the prince of Moravia, Rastislav, in 862 requested missionaries from the Byzantine empire. He wanted missionaries who could teach his people in their native language. The Byzantine emperor, Michael III, responded by sending two brothers, Constantine and Methodius. The brothers met Rastislav's requirements because they were Greeks from Thessalonika (modern-day Macedonia), part of the Byzantine empire that was populated by Slavs.

Constantine created an alphabet and used it to begin translating the Gospels and Greek religious texts. None of these original texts still exist, but they were the first examples of the language that scholars would later call Old Church Slavic.

The two brothers had significant success in Moravia. They introduced the Greek liturgy and attracted many pupils. In 867 they traveled to Rome to seek the pope's approval of their work and to have their pupils ordained to the priesthood. The pope blessed their efforts. While in Rome, Constantine became a monk and took the name Cyril. Cyril died in 869 before leaving Rome.

Methodius returned to Moravia, but in 870 Rastislav's nephew, Svatopluk, overthrew his uncle and allowed Methodius to be imprisoned. He was released in 873, but Svatopluk was hostile to him and his work for the rest of his life. After Methodius' death in 885, all of the Slavic clergy were driven out of Moravia.

Many of the monks and religious scholars from Moravia escaped to Bulgaria, where Czar Boris had accepted Christianity as the official state religion. With the support of the czar, the Slavic literary tradition blossomed, and OCS became the literary language of the Bulgarian capital. This is the literary language and religious tradition that the Russians adopted in 988.

Practice

A. What difference do you think it would have made if Western, such as Irish Catholic, missionaries had been the ones to spread Christianity in Bulgaria?

7.4. Other Ancient Letters

Two variations of Slavic were spoken in the area of present-day European Russia and Ukraine at the end of the first millenium A.D. The commonly used language was Old Russian, written in the Cyrillic alphabet, based mainly on the Greek alphabet and named in honor of Saint Cyril. The second variation in use was employed in services in the Orthodox Church and as a literary language. This language, which greatly resembled Old Russian, was Church Slavic (*церкѡвнославѧн-ский*), a version of Old Church Slavic. Clerics have left a fairly sizable corpus of manuscripts written in Church Slavic. The following selection was written in Church Slavic during the eleventh century A.D. It is from the so-called Turov Gospel.

(19)   Въ врѣмѧ оно въниде іс҃ъ въ капєрнаоумъ въ градъ
       галилєйскъ и бѣ оуча въ сѫботы и оужасахѫ сѧ ученици ієго
       іако съ властиіѫ бѣ слово ієго.

(От Λукы IV, 31–32)

In this selection the word *ісоусъ* "Jesus" is abbreviated to *іс҃ъ*. Some words are recognizable (*Въ, оно, градъ, и, слово,* etc.), even if they are encumbered with jers. Other words look familiar (*врѣмѧ, ієго*). And other words in this selection are unfamiliar to most educated speakers of Russian (*оужасахѫ*, for example).

Practice

A. What letters in this text are not used in modern Russian? What letters does modern Russian use in their place?

B. What is the modern equivalent for the following? Use context to help determine grammatical category, or look it up in a Russian Bible.

1. врѣмѧ	6. оужасахѫ сѧ
2. въниде	7. оученици
3. градъ	8. iего
4. бѣ оучѧ	9. iако
5. сѫботы	10. бѣ

The selection given above is harder to understand than later texts such as "Нáши прéдки," because it differs more radically from modern Russian. In addition to different letters such as *oy* and *ѫ*, both of which are replaced by modern *y*, we are faced with a different set of grammatical endings and a few completely different words. Still, the text provides some important clues to our questions regarding sound alternations in modern Russian. Recall that some consonants are soft before back vowels [y], [o], and [a]. Why? Russian also has an alternation of the type [г] ~ [з] as in *друг ~ друзья*. Why? A spelling rule in Russian contradicts the idea of assimilation; it states that *ы*, a back vowel, is never written or pronounced after the back consonants *к, г, х*; instead we write the front vowel *и*. Why? Older writings such as the Turov Gospel provide clues to these questions.

7.4.1. Ancient Vowels

Recall that paired consonants in the modern language may be hard or soft before the back vowels *o, a,* or *y*. This makes little sense physiologically because only front vowels are candidates for the kind of assimilation that brings about consonant softening. For instances of soft consonants before [o], we have already seen that this [o] has its source in the front vowel [ə] which shifts to [o] under stress and before a hard consonant (*мёд* [м'от] < Old Russian *медъ*).

The excerpt from the Turov Gospel helps us see a similar origin for soft consonants before [a]. Consider the second word from that selection. It equates to the modern Russian *время*. This word is interesting because in the modern language it has a soft consonant followed by a back vowel, namely *мя*, morphologically {врэ́м' +a}. Note the letter in the Old Russian manuscript is not *я*, but *ѧ*. The letter that usually represents *я* in Old Russian is *ia* as in the word *iако* 'because.' We conjecture that the letter *ѧ* represents a different sound, perhaps a front vowel of some kind, since soft consonants precede it. It appears that *ѧ* was a type of front vowel capable of causing softening which later shifted to [a]. A glance at the modern Russian inflectional paradigm of this word gives us a clue to how *ѧ* was pronounced.

(20) Nom   вре́м<u>я</u>
      Gen   вре́м<u>ени</u>
      Prep   вре́м<u>ени</u>
      Dat   вре́м<u>ени</u>
      Inst   вре́м<u>ене</u>м
               etc.

A suffix -*ен*- is present in all the case forms of this word, except the nom sg. We can say that the "ending" of the nom sg -*я* alternates with the suffix -*ен*- throughout the rest of the paradigm. What is particularly interesting about this suffix is that it contains a front vowel. It turns out that *ѧ* is an [ə] with a nasal sound attached to it, like the [ę] in modern French and Polish. We will transcribe this sound as [ə̨], a nasalized front vowel. We can be sure we are dealing with a front vowel since consonants directly preceding it were and are soft. Ultimately nasal vowels were lost in Russian and [ə̨] shifted to [a]. These changes are given in chronological order in (21). The postulated Common Slavic is a reconstructed form, based on information about the word in the modern language. Compare this form with the way it was written in Old and Modern Russian.

(21)   **Common Slavic (postulated):**   в р ѣ м э н

Consonants became soft before front vowels: в р′ ѣ м′ э н

Vowels became nasalized before a nasal cons: в р′ ѣ м′ ӛ н

Nasal consonants were lost after nasal vowels: в р′ ѣ м′ ӛ

Old Russian (attested):   врѣмѧ

Nasal vowels become oral vowels   в р′ ѣ м′ а

Unstressed vowels are reduced (akanje)   в р′ ѣ м′ ъ

Modern Russian (attested):   время

The sequence of sounds [эн] in the Common Slavic form was not just made up to account for the soft quality of the preceding consonant. It can be seen elsewhere in the paradigm of this word, for example, gen sg *времени*. This "internal reconstruction" of Russian, that is, reconstructing what an earlier stage of Russian might have been like by comparing modern word alternations, also suggests that an earlier form of the nom sg of *врéмя* was *времéн*.

The presence of *ѣ* in *врѣмѧ* corresponds to modern *e* as expected. The letter *ѣ* also occurs in (20) in the word *бѣ* 'was.' Other vowel letters are: *o, ъ, e* (=modern *e*), *u, ы*. Another letter which falls at the end of several words is *ѧ*. This letter also occurs in the word *сѧботы* 'Sabbath', modern Russian *суббóта*. Church Slavic *ѫ* was a back nasal vowel which ultimately became *y* in modern Russian. Compare the following words in Church Slavic and in Modern Russian.

(22) **Church Slavic**   **Modern Russian**

грѫбъ   груб

дѫбъ   дуб

живѫтъ   живýт

властиѭ   влáстью

We can be sure that the vowel *ѫ*, however, was a back vowel, since there is no evidence of consonant softening before it. It is transcribed as [ǫ]. The reason some consonants are soft before the back vowel [у], (i.e., богúню [блг′úн′у]), lies elsewhere.

7.5. Change in Meaning

One of the words in the excerpt we have been studying appears to have changed somewhat in meaning since its writing. Consider the following clause from the excerpt given above:

(23)   и оужасахѫ сѧ оученици іего

'and his disciples were astonished'

This clause differs greatly from Modern Russian (MR). The conjugated verb, *оужасахѫ*, contains a recognizable root: *оужас* (cf. MR *у́жас*), and the following vowel resembles the MR verbal suffix seen in verbs like *чита́ть*, but the ending -*хѫ*- does not resemble any modern Russian ending. This verb is the precursor of MR *ужаса́ться* 'to be horrified, terrified.' It seems likely that this was not the meaning of this verb in Church Slavic. Instead the word meant something like 'to be astonished, amazed.' The ways and direction of shifts in meanings (semantic shifts) constitute an entire discipline in linguistics: semasiology (*семасиоло́гия*). We will limit ourselves here to noticing that this is one important and as yet poorly understood way in which languages change over time.

7.6. Velar Palatalization

The third word in (23) is the reflexive particle, where we see the letter ѧ for MR я, i.e., *сѧ* = *ся*. The fourth word has the letter ц in the nom pl form. The nom sg is *оученикъ*. This presents us with the phonological alternation к ~ ц, one that can still be seen in modern Russian:

(24)   каба́к 'tavern'   каба́цкий 'coarse, vulgar'

       каза́к 'Cossack'   каза́цкий 'Cossack (adj.)'

       восклики́кнуть 'exclaim'   восклица́ть 'exclaim (imperf.)'

       о́блик 'face, appearance'   лицо́ 'face'

(25)   княги́ня 'princess'   князь 'prince'

       друг 'friend'   друзья́ 'friends'

These and other words like those illustrated in (24) and (25) suggest earlier phonological alternations: к ~ ц′, ӡ ~ ӡ′. The shift of к and ӡ to ц and ӡ, respectively, occurred twice in the development of Russian. The first instance, usually called "the progressive velar palatalization," took place during the early Common Slavic period, though the absolute and relative chronology of the progressive palatalization continues to be debates. Up to now we have only seen regressive phonological shifts, where the second of two adjacent sounds affects the first. In the progressive velar palatalization, the sound u affected a following velar (к or ӡ), if an a, o, or y immediately followed. This shift occurred even if a sonorant intervened between the u and the velar. Thus from *kuningas 'king' and *atikas 'father' developed Old Russian кънязь and отьць. The front jers at the end of each word suggest that the ӡ and ц were soft.

The results of a separate but closely related velar palatalization were similar to those of the progressive palatalization, that is к → ц and ӡ → ӡ. In addition in this sound change x → c. This shift occurred before front vowels, including ѣ, thus отрокъ 'boy' is отроцѣ in the prep sg and рѫка 'arm' is рѫцѣ in the prep sg. The attested form оученици is due to this velar palatalization.

In the modern language these alternations do not occur in paradigms (except in друг~друзья), and only occasionally across word forms (as in (24) and (25) above). The final stem consonant found in most cases in the paradigm, including the nom, has been generalized throughout: now ученик ~ об ученике, ученики. A few traces remain of the old system: друг ~ друзья, for instance. Varied influences have produced a mosaic in the modern language, where these kinds of alternations occur sporadically. It is important, however, to see that modern ц has its origins in к, and thus occasionally appears to alternate with ч: отец ~ отеческий, улица ~ уличный.

We now turn our attention to a sound change that had far reaching effects in the modern language. The so-called **first regressive velar palatalization** is responsible for the ч in у_ч_еник (with the same historical root as found in нау_к_а). Also a very early shift, this sound change may be expressed:

(26)   Regressive Velar Palatalization   к, г, х → ч′, ж′, ш′ __ v̈
(v̈ = front vowel)

The rule in (26) states that velars became palatalized hushers before a front vowel. Another way of saying this is that velars became fronted before front vowels (assimilation). The final result of becoming fronted was that they mutated to hushers.

It is not simply by chance that the sounds involved in this rule are all velars. Instead we observe a general tendency for back (hard) consonants to be fronted before front vowels. It is natural that these newly formed hushers were pronounced soft since they resulted from a fronting (softening) process. We know that subsequently *ш*, *ж*, and *ц* underwent velarization or hardening (*отвердéние*). Janovich presents evidence for when this latter change took place in Russian.

> Шипящие [ш], [ж], [ч], [ц] были в древнерусском языке исконно мягкими, так как они возникли в результате палатализации заднеязычных еще в праславянскую эпоху. В дальнейшем в истории языка происходит их отвердение (за исключением [ч′], которое, однако, развивалось не одновременно и не одинаково в восточнославянских диалектах).
>
> Наиболее достоверные свидетельства отвердения шипящих—написание [ы] вместо [и] после шипящих. Такие написания отмечаются с XIV в.: слышышь (1300г.) жывите, держыть (до 1389 г.). Следы отвердения [ц′] появляются позднее, с конца XV в.: улыцы (1499 г.), концы (XVI в.). О позднем отвердении [ц′] свидетельствует и тот факт, что перед этим согласным звук [э] не изменился в [о].

Practice

A. In what way does the pronunciation of modern hushers and *ц* differ from the way they were pronounced a thousand years ago?

B. Why doesn't stressed *é* shift to *ó* before a *ц* (example *отéц*)?

Since all hushers were soft it would have been redundant to write *ю* and *я* after them, and for that reason we find *у* and *а* written after hushers. After the hushers became hard any possible reason for writing *ю* and *я* after them disappeared. It is also important to note that hushers, unlike other consonants, were never paired for palatalization.

Therefore, the vowels that followed them did not need to carry information about palatalization and could be represented by the unmarked letter.

One of the front vowels which triggered the first regressive palatalization of velars was ѣ. We saw earlier that in most instances this sound shifted to *e*: OR *снѣгъ* → MR *снег*. However, **when following a husher** ѣ shifted to *a*: Proto-Slavic *крикѣти* → *кричѣти* → MR *кричáть*. Because of this shift, modern Russian has *a* following hushers as in *слы́шать, отличáть, звучáть*, etc., when there is no evidence of earlier front vowel plus nasal, as in *начáть / начнý*, which implies *начáти / начьнý*.

Today the hushers ч and щ retain their palatalized characteristics but the other hushers have hardened; when the latter are pronounced, the body of the tongue is raised toward the roof of the mouth, rather than toward the ridge in the front of the mouth. V. V. Ivanov places the hardening of [ш] and [ж] at the end of the fourteenth century and the hardening of [ц] during the sixteenth century. We represent the hardening of the hushers and ц:

(27)   a.   ш′, ж′, ц′ → ш, ж, ц

or simply as

(27)   b.   Č′ → Č (where Č ≠ ч,щ)

In the modern language ы is not written after hushers because all hushers were once soft and followed by *u*. After ш and ж became hard, any *u* following these consonants assimilated the back feature from the hushers, i.e., began to be pronounced [ы], but the spelling did not change. The spelling *has* changed, however, after ц: *ýлицы*. With the exception of ц, for consonants not paired for palatalization, *u* seems to have been interpreted as the unmarked letter of the pair *u* and *ы*. This is similar to the point made earlier about *a* and *y* after husher. We will have more to say about this later.

The sound changes illustrated by the rules in (26) and (27) account for the distribution of stem final hushers in 2nd conj verbs. Verbs with the suffix *-u(mь)* do not have roots that end in a velar, instead they end in a husher. In other words, there are no verbs in Russian that end:

-гить, -кить, or -хить. Instead they end in -жить, -чить, and -шить. Compare the related words in (28):

(28)　легко́　　but　　облегчи́ть　　'to facilitate'
　　　 су́хо　　　　　　 осуши́ть　　　 'to dry'
　　　 друг　　　　　　 дружи́ть　　　 'to be friends'

This is not to say that velars do not occur before front vowels. Due to analogy they occur before front vowels that are grammatical endings: кни́ги, о подру́ге, ру́ки, пе́ки. Due to a sound change that occurred in the twelfth century, the sound [ы] was no longer possible after velars; it was replaced by the sound [и]: хи́трый, Ки́ев, ги́бкий. Thus, velars may also occur before [и] in roots. With the exception of endings discussed above, the combination of *velar + e: ге, ке, хе* occurs only in borrowed words. Finally, many words have been borrowed into Russian since the rule in (27) ceased being active. Therefore, these borrowings do not reflect the mutation of velars: гимн, кит, хи́мия, and we must account for alternations such as those in (28) by means of a morphophonemic rule.

7.7. Dejotation

The velar palatalizations that we just discussed are very satisfying because they explain so many of the morphophonemic alternations that we see today. We know why the root {ук} has two different forms, e.g., in нау́ка, нау́чный. The latter would have been Proto Slavic наукьный. Of course, in strictly synchronic terms, we understand нау́ка and нау́чный to be related by morphophonemic rule:

(29)　нау́ка　　　 {нау́к +а}
　　　 нау́чный　　{нау́ч -*/н +ый}

where the suffix {-*/н} is specified by rule to cooccur with hushers, not velars.

However, not all hushers derive from a velar, and so cannot be explained by the velar palatalizations. And not all hushers derived from velars are from the first regressive velar palatalization.

(30) писа́ть   пишу́   (from *c*, not a velar)

      пла́кать   пла́чу   (no front vowel follows)

      ма́зать   ма́жу   (from *з*, not a velar)

      иска́ть   ищу́   (no front vowel follows)

      рассы́пать   рассы́плю   (mutation of labials!)

We have two problems in explaining these forms. First, there appear to be no front vowels responsible for the observed mutations. Second, this development involved more types of consonants than just velars. This historical development in the Common Slavic and Old Russian consonantal systems is called dejotation (*йота́ция*), and it took place at about the same time and for similar reasons as the velar palatalizations. A simplification of consonant clusters made up of a velar, a dental, or a labial plus *ŭ* took place. This simplification resulted from merging *ŭ* with the consonant before it to form a husher or, in the case of labials, to add an *л'*:

(31) кй > ч'   скй > щ'

      гй > ж'   стй > щ'

      хй > ш'

      сй > ш'   ктй > ч'

      зй > ж'   гтй > ч'

      дй > ж'

      тй > ч'

      мй > мл'   лй > л'

      бй > бл'   нй > н'

      вй > вл'   рй > р'

Note also that South Slavic languages show slightly different results with dejotation, particularly in regard to the sequence *-дŭ-* and *-тŭ-*, which yielded *-жд-* and *-щ-*. This explains Russian *д~ж* (*води́ть ~ вожу́*) as opposed to borrowed *д~жд* (*предупреди́ть ~ предупрежду́*).

The process of dejotation explains many of the consonant alternations that we see in inflectional and derivational morphology.

(32)	махáть	машý	<	мах й у
	чи́стить	чи́щу	<	чист й у
	корóткий	корóче	<	корот й е
	влюби́ть	влюблён	<	влюб й ен
	купи́ть	куплю́	<	куп й у

Historically, then, we can see the following sequence of events:

(33)   пис й у   —(dejotation)→   пиш у

But dejotation is no longer an active, productive process in modern Russian. I-kratkoe can stand after consonants without any change occurring: *съел* 'he ate' [сйэл]. When this phonological rule ceased to operate in Russian, Russians simply learned two forms of the root for 'write', one for the nonpresent and derived forms (*писáть, писáл, писáтель*) and one for conjugation (*пишý, пишýщий*). There is no morphological rule relating these forms. They became suppletive when the rule dejotation ceased to operate.

Practice

A. Now for a real brain bender. What is the source of mutation observed in the pair *просветúть ~ просвéчивать*. To answer correctly, you need to know that *u* shifted to *й* whenever followed by a vowel.

B. What is the difference in the mutations that we observe in *крик ~ кричáть* and *просветúть ~ просвéчивать*?

7.8. A Spelling Rule Mystery

We may now ask why Modern Russian does not allow the spelling of *ы* after velars, requiring *u* instead: *столы́* but *пироги́, рýки*.

In Old Russian just the opposite distribution can be observed in regard to the velars: only *кы, гы, and хы* were written and presumably so pronounced. In the twelfth century, however, documents begin to show that the velars were undergoing some change; they are softened and followed by *u*. And today we can only have *u* (never *ы*) after velars. No one knows for certain why this change, which is opposite to assimilation, occurred.

The shift of [ы] to [и] after velars may be explained on the basis of analogy, the process where one form changes due to pressure of many related forms. In the eleventh century Russian did not have the sequence of sound *к'и*, though other consonants freely combined with *и*: *м'и*, *н'и*, etc. Instead, it had *ц'и* according to the second regressive palatalization of velars. It may be suggested that when the analogical shift of *ц* back to *к* took place (*ученици* → *ученики*) the palatalized quality of the [ц'] may have been retained in connection with [к]: (*ц'* → *к'*). The presence of [к'и] in paradigms may then have served as an analogical basis for the shift of all instances of *кы* to *ки*. This situation may also be connected to the fact, as a pointed out earlier for the hushers, that *и* has been interpreted as the unmarked variant of the pair *и~ы* for consonants not paired for palatalization. Hard and soft velars, unlike dentals and labials, are in complementary distribution. Soft velars never occur with back vowels.

Practice

A. Why do soft consonants occur before the vowels [и] and [э] in Modern Russian?

   Data: ме́сто, миг

B. Why do soft "paired" consonants occur before back vowels [o] and [a]?

   Data: пёк [п'ок], пять [п'ат']

C. Why does Russian have the spelling rule that states *к, г, х* are never followed by *ы*, only by *и*?

   Data: ноги́ [ног'и], за́сухи [засух'и]

7.9. The Loc-2, Gen-2, and Infinitive Endings

Leftovers from an earlier grammatical system sometimes turn up in the modern language as exceptional forms. For example, students of Russian must generally memorize the monosyllabic masc nouns that take the so-called locative- or prep-2 ending -*ý* (*в снегý, в лесý*, etc.). In older texts we see these endings with this group of nouns in cases other than the prep.

In the Novgorod region Old Russian was written on birch bark and many of these writings were preserved underground and in swamps and have been excavated. The following birch bark text was written toward the end of the twelfth century in Novgorod.

(34)   отъ гостаты къ васильви · ієжє ми отьць даалъ и роди
съдаали а то за нимь а нынѣ вода новоую жєноу а мънѣ нє
въдастъ ничьто жє избивъ роукы поустилъ жє ма а иноую
поалъ доеди добрѣ сътвора ·

It may be translated

(35)   From Gost'ata to Vasilii. That which father gave me and
relatives gave is now his. But taking a new wife he will give me
nothing. Having divorced me, he has driven me out and another
(wife) he has taken. Please come.

While this text contains much that is distinct from modern Russian, it is closer to modern Russian than the text in the Turov gospel in several ways. It contains only one nasal vowel letter (*а*, which corresponds to modern Russian *я*), and it is "misspelled" in all words here except *поалъ*, which did have a nasal vowel (cf. *взял ~ возьму*). The nasal vowel letter *ѫ* of Common Slavic has already become the back vowel [y], written *оу*: compare Church Slavic *рѫка* with Old Russian *роука*. This letter contains the same set of jers seen in the earlier two texts. The birch bark writing also contains verbal forms which are similar to the modern language: past tense *съдаали* '(they have) given,' past verbal adverb *избивъ* 'having broken.' The noun endings are also familiar, with the exception of the dat ending after the preposition *къ: васильви*. Modern Russian has the dat ending for this word -*ю: к Василию*. The ending -*ови*, which we see in (34) in its soft variant -*ьви*, comes from another set of endings, which for the most part do not exist in the modern language. This set of endings occurred with the so-called "u-stem nouns," predominantly monosyllabic masc nouns. These nouns are referred to as u-stem nouns, because the set of endings they took featured the vowel sound [y], as in *лесу*, in one form or another, including *ъ, оу, ъви, ове, овъ*.

It is possible to make two kinds of [в] sounds. In the first, the upper teeth touch the lower lips to create a point of articulation resulting in the fricative [ф] and [в]. The other pronunciation of [в] is called bilabial. In it, both lips barely touch each other so that a fricative is created. The bilabial variant was the one used at a very early stage in the development of Russian. Having been derived from Indo-European [u] or [w], it is considered a sonorant, and like other sonorants does not trigger voicing assimilation. The close connection between Indo-European [u] and Slavic [в] can also be seen in a set of endings that occurred in Common Slavic. Traces of these noun endings are still evident in the modern language.

Recall that *ъ* was a very reduced "uh" sound. Here is a full Old Russian paradigm of a u-stem noun, *сынъ* 'son'.

(36)	sg	dual	pl
nom	сынъ	сыны	сынове
acc	сынъ	сыны	сыны
gen	сыноу	сыновоу	сыновъ
loc	сыноу	сыновоу	сынъхъ
dat	сынови	сынъма	сынъмъ
ins	сынъмъ	сынъма	сынъми
voc	сыноу	сыны	сынове

As indicated in (36), Old Russian had in addition to sg and pl another number, namely dual, used when discussing two of a certain item. There was also another case, the vocative (voc) case, used when addressing a person or thing. Nearly all the endings associated with u-stem nouns in Old Russian have been lost. The word *мёд* 'honey', an old u-stem noun, is now declined like *стол*. Some of the u-stem endings, however, have survived, and one has become the normal gen pl ending for masc nouns ending in a hard consonant: *-ов*. Other survivors of the u-stem paradigm can still be found in certain masc nouns in the prep sg and in the gen sg cases. Consider, for example, the forms in (37) and (38):

(37)   о мёде 'about honey'   в меду́ 'in the honey'

       о сне́ге 'about snow'   в снегу́ 'in the snow'

       о ле́се 'about the forest'   в лесу́ 'in the forest'

       о бе́реге 'about the shore'   на берегу́ 'on the shore'

While the spelling is slightly different (Old Russian -*оу*, modern Russian -*у*), the endings seen in the right-hand column of (37), the so-called locative-2 endings, are a leftover from the older u-stem paradigm.

(38)   без до́ма 'without a house'   и́з дому 'from the house'

       без ле́са 'without a forest'   и́з лесу 'from the forest'

       без го́лода 'without hunger'   с го́лоду 'from hunger'

The gen-2 endings on the words in the right column in (38) also show traces of the old u-stem paradigm. This ending has become generalized to form a separate partitive ending for some masc nouns: *са́хару*, *ча́ю, шокола́ду* 'some sugar, some tea, some chocolate', etc. The dat sg ending -*ови*, or as it appears in the text in (34) -*ьви* is no longer used in the modern language. It has been replaced by the normal 1st declension dative ending {+y}.

Older written texts provide direct evidence of language change. While they may not be perfect representations of how a language was spoken they do provide many clues to earlier stages of a given language and are useful in explaining variations in the modern language.

Practice

A. Consider the following data from Modern Russian. If the loc-2 forms represent a remnant of another case, what can we conclude about the endings of that case in 3rd declension fem nouns?

Nom	Prep	Locative-2
связь	о свя́зи	в связи́
глубь	о глу́би	в глуби́
даль	о да́ли	в дали́
кровь	о кро́ви	в крови́
пыль	о пы́ли	в пыли́

B. There are three infinitive endings in Russian: *-ть, -чь, -ти*. The following illustrates these three forms. What do the words in each column have in common that distinguishes them from the words in each of the other two columns? If you are stumped, consider the conjugation of the words in each column.

(1)	читáть	(2)	печь	(3)	нести́
	говори́ть		течь		вести́
	гуля́ть		мочь		идти́
	смотре́ть		бере́чь		ползти́
	лезть		сечь		спасти́

C. Here are several infinitives from Ukrainian, a close relative of Russian: *читати, гуляти, лізти, пекти, текти, могти, берегти, сікти, нести, вести*.

    a. The data in exercise B suggest that at an earlier time Russian may have had only one infinitive ending, namely _____.

    b. What sound events must have occurred in Russian to arrive at the other infinitive endings found in Modern Russian?

    c. Referring to your answer in (a), write out the Common Slavic form of the following three infinitives: *говори́ть, мочь, нести́*. Show the step-by-step sound developments for each.

7.10. The Origin of Fleeting Vowels

Why does Russian have fleeting vowels? In section 7.2.3 we discussed the loss of weak vowels (jers). In the text given in 7.2 jers can be found written only at word final position. In the text in 7.4, jers also occur within words. The fate of the jers in Russian has been called one of the most significant events in the history of the language.

As stated earlier, Old Russian contained two reduced vowels, a front weak vowel (*ерь*) and a back weak vowel (*ер*). The jers were found in endings (nom sg masc *-ъ*, gen pl fem *-ъ*, for example). However, in addition to occurring at word final position, jers were also found within words and in prefixes. Compare the words in the left column of (39), taken from a dictionary of Old Russian, with their modern equivalents.

(39) **Old Russian**   **Modern Russian**

    отьць   отéц

    чьто   что

    лодъка   лóдка

    лодъкъ   лóдок (gen pl)

    мъхъ   мох

    пришьлъ   пришёл

    дьнь   день

    вьсь   весь

    съмыслъ   смысл

    съмьрть   смерть

    жьньць   жнец 'reaper'

As expected, the MR equivalents have lost the final jer. (In the case of *весь*, *день*, and *смерть*, a trace of the jer remains—the softness of the word final consonant.) Note, however, that many of the other jers have become full vowels in modern Russian: ъ has become *o* and ь has become *e*. In addition, these vowels appear to be unstable, that is, these vowels are fleeting vowels in these words, as illustrated by the nom sg *лóдка*, gen pl *лóдок*.

Fleeting vowels originated as jers. Some jers developed into full vowels, others were dropped.

Jers in Old Russian can be categorized into two major groups: (i) jers in strong position and (ii) jers in weak position. Strong jers were those followed by a jer in the **next** syllable. Jers in weak position, or weak jers, came at the end of the word or were followed by a strong jer or a regular vowel in the **next** syllable. Examples (w=weak, s=strong):

(40) р ъ т ъ   с ъ м ь р т ь   с ъ м ы с л ъ

       s w   w s w   w   w

       2 1   3 2 1   1   1

In (40) jers have been numbered starting at the end of the word and working backward. Odd numbered jers are weak and subsequently disappear from the word. Even numbered jers are strong and become full vowels. Notice that if a full vowel intervenes (e.g., *ы* in *съмыслъ*) the counting starts over.

The gen pl form of fem and neut nouns often contains a fleeting vowel because one of the gen pl fem and neut endings was -*ъ*. If the stem ended in a syllable with a jer, then this gen pl ending caused the stem jer to become strong:

(41) **Nom Sg**   поговóрка (= O.R. поговóр‌ъ‌ка)
                                                              w
    Gen Pl   поговóрок (= O.R. поговóр‌ъ‌къ)
                                                              s w

    Nom Sg   окнó (= O.R. ок‌ъ‌нó)
                                                        w
    Gen Pl   óкон (= O.R. óк‌ъ‌нъ)
                                                      s w

The ending -*ъ* was also used for nom sg masc nouns, the masc sg ending for the so-called "*l*-participle" (modern Russian past tense), and for masc sg short form adjectives:

(42) **nom sg masc:** сон   (= O.R. сънъ)
    gen sg: сна   (= O.R. съна)

    l-part. masc: пришёл   (=O.R. пришьлъ)
    l-part. fem: пришлá   (= O.R. пришьла)

    short form masc: бóлен   (= O.R. больнъ)
    short form fem: больнá   (= O.R. больна)

The words in (42) show how a jer could be weak in one case form of the word (when followed by a full vowel) and could be strong in another case form of the word (when followed by a jer).

Practice

A. Write how you think the following were written in Old Russian. Note that each but the last has a "fleeting vowel."

1. лóдка (gen pl лóдок)
2. дéвушка (gen pl дéвушек)
3. совсéм
4. сон (gen sg сна)

5. отéц (gen sg. отцá)
6. окнó (gen pl. óкон)
7. довóлен (fem. довóльна)
8. лес (gen sg. лéса)

7.11. Dialectal Pronunciation of [г]

The pronunciation of *г* is one of the most telling dialectal features of spoken Russian. In the northern and central regions, *г* is pronounced [г] in all positions except word final position where devoicing occurs. In southern regions *г* is pronounced as a voiced [x] (transcribed [γ]) which devoices to [x] at word final position. Examples:

(43)   **Northern/Central**   **Southern**

Northern/Central	Southern
[г]óрод	[γ]óрод
бé[г]ает	бé[γ]ает
дорó[г]а	дорó[γ]а
мнó[г]о	мнó[γ]о
[г]од	[γ]од
твóро[к]	твóро[x]

In standard Russian the gen sg adj ending -*ого* and the pronoun *егó* are pronounced with a [в]: *стáрого* [стá'ръвъ], *сегóдня* [с'ивóд'н'ъ], *егó* [йивó]. In Old Russian these were pronounced with a [г]. When Russians speaking the southern dialect moved into the central region in the thirteenth to fourteenth centuries they brought with them their pronunciation of *г* as [γ]. For unknown reasons this pronunciation was adopted by central Russian speakers—but it has been retained only in the gen sg ending and the pronoun *его*. Since the voiced fricative [γ] was not a sound in the speech of central Russians they substituted the sound that seemed closest, namely the voiced fricative [в]. This pronunciation in these words and in ecclesiastical words, which also reflect a southern influence, such as [γ]*оспóдин, бо*[x] has become standard pronunciation in MR.

V. V. Ivanov relates the following regarding Anna, Queen of France and daughter of Jaroslav the Wise:

> Предполагают также, что о фрикативном образовании [г] на юге древней Руси XI в. свидетельствует подпись французской королевы Анны Ярославны. Дочь Ярослава Мудрого—Анна, вдова Генриха I, выросшая в Киеве, оставила свою подпись, сделанную кириллическими буквами, на одной из латинских грамот 1063 г. Эта подпись состоит из двух слов: **ана ръина**, т.е. Anna regina—«Анна королева». В слове regina пропущена буква g, что, возможно, связано с чуждостью для Анны взрывного образования [g] латинского языка. Именно на этом основании и предполагают, что в XI в. в Киеве уже был [γ]. Однако это основание не может считаться достаточно веским, так как в написании **ръина** может отражаться старофранцузское произношение данного слова *reine* «королева».

7.12. Review

In order to understand why certain phenomena occur in modern Russian we have resorted to a brief excursus into its history. We found that many irregularities in the modern language resulted from historical sound changes (for instance, *врѣмен* → *врема* → *врéмя*). Spelling rules find their origin in historical sound shifts (for instance, *u* is written after *ш* and *ж* because the latter were once soft). We discover that the shift of stressed [э] to [о] before hard consonants was a simple case of assimilation, with [э] assimilating the [–front] feature of hard consonants. Through comparison with other related languages and dialects we learn how certain Russian letters, which are no longer written, might have been pronounced. The historical development of reduced vowels, the jers, is the basis for modern fleeting vowels. The sound changes discussed in this chapter are outlined below.

Sound Change	Description	Sect
K → Ц′ / v̈ __ a,y,o	progressive velar palatalization	7.6
K → Ч′ / __ v̈	1st regressive velar palat.	7.6 (26)
C → C′ / __ v̈	consonant softening	2.1.5
v̈N → A / __ #, C	nasalization of vowels	7.4.1
A → a /everywhere	loss of nasal vowels	7.4.1
K → Ц′ / __ и, ѣ	2nd regressive velar palat.	7.6
т, д, с... → ч, ж, ш ...	dejotation	7.7
TORT → TOROT	full vocalization	7.3
Č′ → Č /everywhere	hardening of ж, ш, ц	7.6 (27)
ъ, ь → о, э / strong	vocalization of jers	7.1
ъ, ь → Ø / weak	loss of weak jers	7.1
э́ → о́ / __ C (hard)	velarization of э́	7.2.1
ѣ → a / Č __	loss of diphthong/long vowel	7.6
ѣ → э / elsewhere	loss of dipthtong/long vowel	7.2.1

Understanding the reasons behind irregularities in the modern language can help students remember them more easily. But an understanding of the principles of sound change can also help uncover simplicity and order in the declensional and conjugational systems and when combined with concepts of morphology allow for a systematic and cohesive description of the language.

Practice

A. Here are a few words as they might have been pronounced in Proto-Slavic. How is each pronounced today? What sound changes can you recognize in the historical development of these words?

1. ръть	6. кьто
2. лодъка	7. лѣсъ
3. несъ	8. дьнь
4. накьнти	9. пришьла
5. улика	10. пришьлъ

B. Using the summary of the rules above, trace the historical development of the following words. Indicate at what point in history the observed changes became morphophonemic or suppletive.

1. тёмный	4. грéшный	7. кричáть	10. люблю́
2. снег	5. скажý	8. кричý	11. козёл
3. день	6. корóче	9. замечáть	12. начнý

This text has pursued the description of Russian from a cognitive point of view. That is, it has taken as axiomatic the suggestion that to model what speakers/hearers of Russian know, a grammar can only make use of information available to those speakers/hearers. We began by describing the sounds of Russian and how sounds interact with each other. In addition, we suggested that literate Russians are able to fashion pronunciation rules based on how Russian is written. We reproduced those rules in matrices that relate groups of sounds and writing to sounds. We found that by applying these rules to endings and by using morphological transcription, we were able to see order in the apparent chaos of noun, verb, and adjective endings. Using these same kinds of tools, we were able to relate alternations between semantically related words in a systematic way and discover morphophonemic processes in Russian. Finally, we made a rapid tour through the main historical sound events that created the language we use today. We found that when a phonological rule ceases to operate, then speakers continue to use words as if that rule were still in operation, but only in words where it was formally used, not in new words. As long as some regularity exists with these words, then a morphophonemic rule continues to relate that regularity to the words involved. When even these more restricted regularities are altered or disappear, then changes brought about by earlier phonological rules become fossilized elements of the language (suppletions). This diachronic and synchronic description of Russian provides a coherent cognitive view of the intricacies of Russian phonology, morphology, and word formation and provides a useful framework for understanding how these have evolved.

REFERENCES

English-Language Sources:

Bybee, Joan. (2001) *Phonology and language use.* Cambridge: Cambridge University Press. [*Cambridge Studies in Linguistics, 94.*]

Langacker, Ronald. (2000) *Foundations of cognitive grammar*, v. 1: *Theoretical prerequisites.* Stanford, CA: Stanford University Press.

Postal, Paul M. (1972) "The best theory." Stanley Peters, ed. *Goals of linguistic theory.* Englewood Cliffs, NJ: Prentice-Hall.

Shteinfeldt, E. (1962) *Russian Word Count.* Moscow: Progress Publishers.

Taylor, John R. (2002) *Cognitive grammar.* Oxford: Oxford University Press.

Russian-Language Sources:

Аванесов, Р. И. 1972. *Русское литературное произношение.* Москва: Просвещение.

Акишина, А. А. и С. А. Барановская. (1980) *Русская фонетика.* Москва: Русский Язык.

Аношин, А. В. «Конспект лекций по русскомы языку.» http://www.gumfak.ru/russ_html/rus_konspekt/content.shtml

Бетенькова, Надежда Михайловна. (1994) *Орфография, граммати-ка—в рифмовках занимательных.* Москва: Просвещение.

Иванов, Валерий Васильевич. (1990) *Историческая грамматика русского языка.* Москва: Просвещение.

Лебедева, Юлия Георгиевна. (1986) *Учитесь говорить правильно.* Москва: Высшая школа.

Мельниченко, Г. Г. (1984) *Хрестоматия по русской диалектологии.* Москва: Просвещение.

Толстой, Лев Никовлаевич. (1968) *Война и мир*. Москва: Художественная литература.

Успенский, М. Б. in www.butuzici.ru/stihi-schitalochki-skorogovorki/chastushkiposlovitsypogovorki/1156--.html

Янович, Б. И. (1986) *Историческая грамматика русского языка*. Минск: Университетское.